The Vision of Robert Flaherty

On location during the making of *Louisiana Story*.

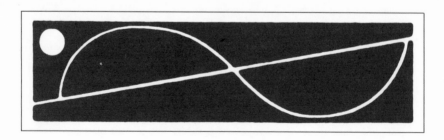

THE

VISION

OF

ROBERT FLAHERTY

The Artist as Myth and Filmmaker

Richard Barsam

INDIANA UNIVERSITY PRESS
BLOOMINGTON AND INDIANAPOLIS

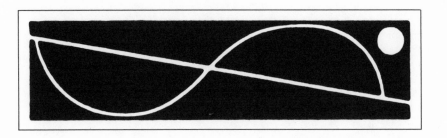

Manufactured in the United States of America

Library of Congress Cataloging-in-Publication Data

Barsam, Richard Meran.
   The vision of Robert Flaherty

   Bibliography: p.
   Includes index.
   1. Flaherty, Robert Joseph, 1884–1951—Criticism
and interpretation.   2. Moving-pictures, Documentary—
Production and direction.   I. Title.
PN1998.A3F466   1988   791.43'0233'0924   87-45488
ISBN 0-253-32074-7
ISBN 0-253-20460-7 (pbk.)

I   2   3   4   5   92   91   90   89   88

In Memory of Mark Berman

Three requisites for a work of art: validity of the myth, vigour of belief, intensity of vocation. . . . The strength of belief in a myth whose validity is diminishing will not produce such a great art as the strength of belief in one which is valid, and none is valid today. Yet no myth is ever quite worthless as long as there remains one artist to lend it his faith.

—CYRIL CONNOLLY
The Unquiet Grave

Contents

x   Contents

A study of the films of Robert Flaherty involves many different subjects: biography, ethnography, geography, the political and cultural features of several of the world's most remote areas, filmmaking techniques and their development from Flaherty's first work in 1913 to his last in 1948, the evolution of nonfiction film theory, specific accomplishments in the nonfiction film genre, and the issues of commercial distribution of nonfiction film, among many others. Since a book of this size cannot hope to deal with all of these subjects except in the most general way, nor can an author hope to be equally expert in all of them, the scope of this study has had of necessity to be somewhat limited. The main point of view of this study is that of the historian and critic of nonfiction film, and I have directed it at those who wish to know more about the relation of Flaherty to his time, the nature of his originality, his working methods, the films themselves, and the importance of his *oeuvre* in the overall development of nonfiction film.

Until the 1970s, Flaherty studies had tended toward the celebration of the legend rather than toward an examination of its sources or an assessment of its validity. The evaluation of Flaherty's work has been especially difficult, not because of the complex or enigmatic nature of the films, but because his name has been unalterably interwoven with the myth that grew about it. A new direction in Flaherty studies was marked by the work of two critics. Richard Corliss' "Robert Flaherty: The Man in the Iron Myth" (1973) began a re-examination of the Flaherty legend, and Jay Ruby (1980) called for its "demystification." Meanwhile, William T. Murphy's *Robert Flaherty: A Guide to References and Resources* (1978) provided an invaluable and objectively annotated bibliography. Although Paul Rotha's *Robert J. Flaherty: A Biography* (ed. Jay Ruby, 1983) contributed a more reliable biography than that of Arthur Calder-Marshall, the need for a scholarly biography remains.

To a certain extent, this book continues the work begun by Corliss and Ruby. It is not a biography, but a critical assessment of Flaherty's approach, working methods, and achievements. It rests on the simple proposition that no matter how hard we try to separate an artist and his work, the two inform each other. One of my purposes is to examine and assess both the form and content of Flaherty's films with the intention of understanding more fully their truth and beauty. Seeing more clearly the merits of Flaherty's films will help us to understand more fully his achievements.

Although each of his films is different, and they do not collectively represent some larger vision of the world, they can be connected through recurring motifs. Flaherty moved from film project to project, exploring and experimenting, never really finding what he wanted or (had he found it) the most satisfactory means to express it. In my view, Flaherty's search had more value than his discovery. To encompass his range of expression, my method has been to study the films with as fresh an approach as possible, to consider not only their humanism and cinematographic realism, but also their formal and technical qualities, and to locate them within the origins and development of the American nonfiction film and, where relevant, the Griersonian documentary film.

All of the films that Flaherty had a direct hand in making are discussed: (1) those that he signed himself: *Nanook of the North* (1922), *Moana: A Romance of the Golden Age* (1926), *Man of Aran* (1934), *The Land* (1942), and *Louisiana Story* (1948); (2) those that he signed in collaboration with others: *Tabu: A Story of the South Seas* (1931, with F. W. Murnau), *Industrial Britain* (1933, with John Grierson), and *Elephant Boy* (1937, with Zoltan Korda); and (3) those that are largely experimental studies: *The Potterymaker* (1925) and *Twenty-Four Dollar Island* (1927). Brief discussion or mention is also given to *White Shadows in the South Seas* (1929), which he quit; *Guernica* (1949), an unfinished study of Picasso's mural; *The Titan: The Story of Michelangelo* (1949) and *St. Matthew Passion* (1951), films by other directors to which Flaherty lent the publicity value of his name as producer. Not included in this study are Flaherty's unrealized film projects; his radio programs for the British Broadcasting Corporation; his novels or autobiographical and general writings.

ACKNOWLEDGMENTS

This book began over ten years ago with the idea of taking a fresh look at Robert Flaherty's films. During its preparation and writing, I was fortunate in receiving a great deal of assistance and encouragement, and it is a pleasure to thank those individuals and institutions who helped me in so many different ways.

To the graduate students in my seminar on Robert Flaherty at The College of Staten Island of The City University of New York, I owe very special thanks for listening to, and helping me to form, many of the opinions expressed here.

The libraries in New York City are particularly rich in Flaherty resources, and I am grateful to the efficient staff members of those institutions that made my research possible: the New York Public Library, and the libraries of the Museum of Modern Art, The College of Staten Island, and Columbia University. I owe warm thanks to Frances Marino and Mimi Woods for organizing and typing research materials; to Richard Avedon, who graciously permitted me to reproduce his portrait of Robert Flaherty; and to the PSC-CUNY Research Award Program for a grant that supported the research.

As he has for twenty years, my friend Charles Silver, at the Film Study Center of the Museum of Modern Art, made my work easier with his usual humor, enthusiasm, and care.

Special thanks are due Charles Affron, Jeffrey Burke, Jack C. Ellis, Edgar Munhall, and Kenneth Robson for reading the first draft and making many helpful suggestions for improving it, and to Helen Van Dongen for her wise counsel.

To my colleague and friend, Brenda Spatt, I owe a deep debt of gratitude for her patient and intelligent editing.

I am grateful to Edgar Munhall for his constant encouragement throughout this endeavor and for understanding how much it meant to me to complete this book.

CHAPTER ONE

The Explorer as Artist

I

When Robert Flaherty died in 1951 in his sixty-seventh year, he had attained a high level of critical and public recognition as a filmmaker and become a legend in cinema history. With five films *(Nanook of the North, Moana: A Romance of the Golden Age, Man of Aran, The Land, Louisiana Story)* that have had a major influence on the development of the American nonfiction film, his achievement was greatly valued by British, European, and American filmmakers, historians, theorists, and critics alike. Although he was a romantic in almost every aspect of his life and art, he influenced many realist filmmakers—Arne Sucksdorff, John Huston, Richard Leacock, Fred Zinnemann, among them. John Grierson listed Flaherty, Méliès, Griffith, Sennett, and Eisenstein as the five great innovators in the history of film. Andrew Sarris chose Flaherty as the sole nonfiction filmmaker in his pantheon of fourteen directors (42–43). Kevin Brownlow, who believes that Flaherty was as important to the nonfiction film as D. W. Griffith was to fiction film, has referred to the "extraordinarily inspirational quality" of his films (471). Jean Renoir wrote: "He was a man made of love. That is why he had so much feeling for the characters in his films. He loved them, that is all" (184). Siegfried Kracauer emphasized the thematic and affective power of the films, praising their "singular beauty" and their "sensitivity to the slow interaction between man and nature, man and man" (204). Thus, by the late 1960s, Robert Flaherty's stature seemed secure, his name enshrined with those of the greatest directors in cinema history.

However, as is often the case with artists, Flaherty's career, full of wondrous questioning and courageous exploration of the world, was marked by alternating success and failure. It was, therefore, inevitable that, after his death, critics would continue to reassess his career and influence. Because Flaherty was a seminal figure in cinema history, his reputation had developed into a myth of some proportions. According to Jay Ruby (66–

73), this myth grew from the self-image Flaherty expressed in his own writings and interviews; the dedicated work of his wife, Frances, in helping to create as well as to nurture the myth; and the efforts of biographers Richard Griffith (1953) and Arthur Calder-Marshall (1963) to promulgate the myth. Taken together, these efforts created images of Flaherty as an explorer; a teller of tales; an intuitive artist who did not preconceive; a maverick, independent film artist; and even the father of the documentary film.[1]

These images require us to imagine a rather singular artist, a supremely romantic figure, the master of a unique destiny. Today we see that, on the contrary, Flaherty's career as a filmmaker was a series of adaptations to odd circumstances, both of temperament and of event, that kept him from conforming to the aesthetic conventions that he dreaded and, thus, from being easily classified. Blessed with an abundant enthusiasm for life, Flaherty loved to explore and to make films, and he worked with whatever approach seemed appropriate, including intuition, preconception, and improvisation. While the Lumière brothers must be credited with making the first nonfiction films, and John Grierson is regarded as the father of the documentary film, Robert Flaherty was among the first filmmakers to observe and record actual life, creating a nonfiction genre all his own. From his close observation and rich imagination, he loved to create stories, both to recount aloud for his friends and to put on film for his audiences. Flaherty was in love with man and the natural world, fascinated with the crafts of primitive man, and appalled by the dehumanizing technology of modern man. He was an idealistic, innocent, and independent artist who fought the establishment with a naive belief in the transcendency of art over money. He was shrewd, realistic, stubborn, decent, and generous, both respected and loved by his contemporaries. Robert Flaherty's passport to distinction was the combination of determined independence and romantic vision that inspired his unique films.

II

Robert Flaherty, the first of seven children, was born on 16 February 1884 in Iron Mountain, Michigan. His mother, Susan Kloeckner, was German and Roman Catholic; his father, Robert Henry Flaherty, a Protestant, emigrated from Ireland by way of Quebec. Young Flaherty, who was raised in the Protestant faith of his father, was too restless to pay much attention to formal learning, and what most boys learned of adventure from books or in

Robert Flaherty, at about age 20, in a portrait made when he
was living in Port Arthur, Ontario, on the northern side of
Lake Superior.

school, Flaherty learned firsthand from the magnificent American frontier and its rugged people.

Of his beginnings, Flaherty said: "First I was an explorer; then I was an artist."[2] As an explorer, his first experiences were the frequent trips accompanying his father searching for iron ore in Minnesota, Michigan, and Canada. In 1910, when he was 26, Flaherty set out on his own to explore for iron ore deposits in the Canadian and sub-Arctic wilderness. Soon he discovered Eskimo life, which fascinated him more than minerals, and by the time he was ready to make his fifth trip in 1920, his aspiration was to make a film about Eskimos and to be an artist.[3] On that trip, Nanook, the legendary hero of that first film, *Nanook of the North* (1922), agreed to Flaherty's request to perform for the camera. "Yes, yes," Nanook said, "the aggie [Eskimo word for motion picture] will come first" (quoted in Ruby 66). For the rest of Robert Flaherty's life, as he traveled to six continents to make films about people who fascinated him, motion pictures came first.

Flaherty's description of himself as the explorer-artist shaped both his life and his art, yet this self-identification was sufficiently ambiguous to allow for a variety of interpretations. His films resist generic classification, and the conventional terms—realist, ethnographic, documentary—do not altogether apply. He was not associated for more than a brief period with any particular nonfiction film movement, nor was he concerned (as, for example, was John Grierson or Pare Lorentz) with film theory. However, his determined individualism and his belief that his art came first provide touchstones for a study of his films.

Flaherty's career was paradoxical in many ways. During his lifetime, the style of the American motion picture evolved constantly, yet the distinguishing characteristics of Flaherty's work remained virtually unchanged from *Nanook of the North* in 1922 to *Louisiana Story* in 1948. Flaherty began his career when filmmakers were self-taught, and he remained true throughout that career to the simple practices that he painstakingly learned through the failures and successes of personal experience. Those techniques that worked for him successfully in making *Nanook* would, he seems to have assumed, continue to serve him well throughout his career.[4] Thus, while his career bridged the transition from silent to sound production, and while he was actively interested in technological improvements made to cameras, lenses, and film stocks, Flaherty was only peripherally interested in the developments in sound recording and editing. John Grierson observed that Flaherty's inflexibility invariably worked against him:

> He remained something of a Sunday painter. He wouldn't learn, or rather he wouldn't work at learning. Sometimes I thought he was too grand to learn

or too indolent to learn. But that was not really the secret. . . . He just hated to conform to the disillusionments of the practical world and especially of the film world in which the practicalities of sponsorship could be more than ordinarily disillusioning. (quoted in Rotha and Wright, "Flaherty Biography Mss." 12–13)

As a cinematographer, Flaherty had a gift for what John Szarkowski calls "photographic seeing."[5] His images were based on actual subject matter that was not easily posed, and he had a great eye for detail, preferring long-focus lenses over short-focus lenses,[6] which he believed produced an image with greater texture and gradations of black and white. (Although he never shot a film on color stock, he followed with interest the developments in color photography.) The long-focus lens preserves the illusion of actual spatial arrangements, increases the possibilities for composition within the frame, and, thus, enhances the dramatic potential of the action photographed by eliminating the non-essential information that accrues through sequences of conventionally edited shots. In landscape shots, he preferred the classic pictorial composition that placed the horizon either high or low in the frame, never in the middle. In close-ups of people, images with which he excelled, he preferred to suggest character and seldom shot full-face. He believed in tantalizing, even puzzling, the audience, and thus seldom relied on the conventional sequence of the establishment shot followed by medium shots and close-ups. When asked what the audience would get from *Man of Aran,* he replied: "Wanting to know more" (quoted by Goldman in Rotha, ed. Ruby, 329).

As a filmmaker, Flaherty relied on his intuition, yet he often did not trust either his intuition, his eye, his material, his colleagues, or his audience. While he disliked the commercial film industry—it had not been kind to him—he respected the motion picture marketplace and knew what the distributors would buy. He shrewdly recognized that traditional audiences generally accepted all nonfiction films, including his own, as valid and reliable documents of actual life. But his temperament and the skills he learned to cope with the wilderness did not equip Flaherty to deal with the businessmen in the film industry, who were as savage as anything he had encountered on six continents; he compared his stay in Hollywood to "going through a sewer in a glass-bottomed boat."[7] As Rotha (ed. Ruby 277) suggests, Flaherty was an uneasy citizen of the world, increasingly out of step with an increasingly irritable industry. Occasionally, Flaherty conformed to industry expectations, but he became more and more independent in a medium that is fundamentally collaborative, and, perhaps, as a result, he suffered from his poor relations with some colleagues and from near-disastrous financial crises stemming from these partnerships. Although he remained at heart a silent filmmaker, he finally accepted montage and sound as integral parts of his work, and *Louisiana Story,* his last film, was also a fully collaborative project and his most sophisticated film. Despite this progress, however, he remained rather oblivious to financial matters. Flaherty had very commercial instincts, but he was one of those persons who are genuinely and temperamentally incapable of understanding money, and had no idea whatsoever where it came from or where it went. The situation worsened over the years, gradually forcing him to relinquish whatever notions of creative and economic independence he may have had in the beginning.

III

While Flaherty did not leave a formal philosophy of life or art, his vision of physical and human nature, a vision which tends to transform reality rather than affirm it, can be found in major themes that recur in his films: natural beauty, older traditions, conflicts between man and nature, families enduring together, knowledge through suffering, a longing for the past. Perhaps central among these is what Siegfried Kracauer calls "the flow of life":

> As a motif pure and simple the flow of life materializes in films animated by no intention other than to picture some manifestation of it. . . . Flaherty's "slight narratives" portray or resuscitate modes of existence that obtain among primitive peoples. . . . Most Flaherty films are expressive of his romantic desire to summon, and preserve for posterity, the purity and "majesty" [Flaherty's word] of a way of life not yet spoiled by the advance of civilization. (273–74)

Flaherty's love of nature, pure and majestic, is cited also by Harold Clurman:

> Flaherty's genius lies in his effort to rediscover nature, so to speak, at its source. This does not imply softness or sentimentality. Struggle and pain are always present in nature and Flaherty observes these with just as patient and loving an eye as its more smiling aspects. In all Flaherty's films nature is shown in its fathomless loveliness, mystery, and grandeur, together with people toiling to live within the pull of its fierce dialectics.[8]

In "Robert J. Flaherty: 1884–1951," Helen Van Dongen, Flaherty's editor on *The Land* and *Louisiana Story,* wrote that "Flaherty liked to settle down where life was peaceful and where he could concentrate on what was graceful and beautiful, turning away from all that was ugly in the world"

(219). These assessments help us to understand his lifelong fascination with the primitive, with the way things used to be (before industrialization), as well as his disregard (at least on film) of contemporary social, political, and economic issues.

All of Flaherty's films are variations on one ideal: happiness exists when man is free and lives simply and harmoniously with nature. Inevitably, however, there must be conflict and, in order to affirm the ascendancy of the human spirit, Flaherty concentrates on conflicts between man and nature rather than those between men. Nature thus serves both as a central motif and as a main character, symbolized by the animal and natural forces that co-exist with man but are also his antagonists. Almost every film has such an antagonist, expressed as a controlling metaphor: *Nanook* (snow, the sea and storms, wild animals); *White Shadows in the South Seas* and *Tabu: A Story of the South Seas* (the sea); *Man of Aran* (the sea and storms); *The Land* (drought, wind, dust storms); *Louisiana Story* (alligators and oil). In *Louisiana Story* (sponsored by the Standard Oil Company), industrialization is portrayed in ways that suggest a force that is both benign and beneficial. It is typical of Flaherty's reverence for living creatures that, in all the films, man's survival is threatened more by weather and the natural elements than by conflict with animals or other men.

In the western humanist's spirit, Flaherty takes human nature as his central theme, celebrates the dignity of man, and makes man the measure of all things. When, inevitably, he must confront nature, man survives by using the skills learned through intuition and tradition. The male protagonists of his films (specifically Nanook, Moana, the men of Aran, the farmers in *The Land,* Mr. Latour in *Louisiana Story)* are masters of nature who survive through their skills as hunters, fighters, and fishermen. Awed by their determination and success, Flaherty idolizes his heroes. Through them, he exalts man's freedom to live as part of nature and demonstrates that those aspects that tie man to nature (his body, his needs, his sensations) are essential to him to the point that he cannot ignore them or be released from them. Flaherty's films explore these ideas as much as they affirm them.

Flaherty's world is centered on his competent heroes and dominated by them. But it is man's reliance on the family unit that sustains and encourages him in his struggle with nature, that gives him a reason for that struggle, especially when it involves hunting for food, and that rewards him with the quiet and lasting pleasures of companionship and love. Domestic and wild animals also serve an important function in Flaherty's films, reminding man of the interdependence of all living creatures as well as of his dependence on nature. When concerned with the relations between men and women, Flaherty presents the individuals or families as types, except in *The Land,* where he tries to suggest the plight of a whole group, rather than a family. Flaherty himself traveled and spent much of his time with his wife and daughters, who were dear to him; nevertheless, in his films, he emphasized the recurring motif of fathers and sons rather than women. Although Frances Flaherty was her husband's collaborator (both official and informal) on his major films (except *Nanook of the North* and *Industrial Britain*), the women in Flaherty's films remain subordinate to their husbands. That is not to say that these women lack character— Nanook's wife Nyla and Maggie in *Man of Aran* are notable for their courage and loyalty—but rather that most of them lack any individual distinction in either characterization or portrayal.

Flaherty's families, living and enduring together, are also the unit in which children learn traditions and grow into adults. As it was in his own youth, education and wisdom are not found in schools or books, but in following family tradition, a father's (not a mother's) example. In his cinematic world, childhood and adolescence include certain rites of initiation by which boys are inducted into the family, the society, and the larger culture of which these units are a part. Flaherty sought out those alien (and sometimes older) cultures that determined the social status of a young man by the nature of the ordeal to which he had submitted himself in adolescence. Through various ritualized ordeals (e.g., in the tattooing scene in *Moana,* the moments of epiphany in *Man of Aran,* the awareness of an adult world and reality in *Elephant Boy* or *Louisiana Story*), these young men do everything possible to end their reliance on the everyday patterns of their youth and break through, not only to adulthood, but also to an understanding of the rhythms of nature and man's place in it. The boy heroes of these films have a quality that helps them transcend daily existence; they seem to *know* the truths necessary for life.

IV

Essentially, Flaherty's films are marked by two traits: his gift as a teller of tales and his achievement of a personal form of cinematic realism greatly admired by André Bazin.[9] Although his method of developing the narrative was not wholly fixed, he followed a predictable pattern, first settling down in the locality to assimilate the everyday life of the people who lived there, then making friends and earning their confidence, and finally beginning to shoot. When he had a script prepared by others (as in *Elephant Boy* or *The Land*), he often overlooked it in favor of his direct perceptions. He spent a long time on location making his films, exchanging one conception for another and, therefore, photographing everything. He wished to be integrated into those societies that were the subjects of his films, so that he might arrive at a record of lives that was truthful to his vision, whether he expressed that truth through actual or restaged footage.

Although Flaherty's narrative gift is the principal strength of his art, it creates a paradoxical and predictable tension between cinematic form and content. Just as Robert Flaherty searched for iron ore, convinced that the mineral was there for the finding, so he approached filmmaking with the similar self-assurance that a story would be there for the finding. In describing her husband's approach to filmmaking, Frances Flaherty used the term "non-preconception": "Non-preconception is the pre-condition to discovery, because it is a state of mind. When you do not preconceive, then you go about finding out. There is nothing else you can do. You begin to explore" (*Odyssey* 10). However, an examination of Flaherty's working methods suggests that his "non-preconception" was not entirely pure. Indeed, preconceptions about people and cultures led him to alter physical and temporal reality in his films. Whether or not he was pleased with what he found in his travels, he succeeded in making it conform cinematically to his own view of the world. Claude Lévi-Strauss says that "the moment that the anthropologist appears on the scene a pristine culture ceases, by definition to be what it was and becomes something else again in order to accommodate the researcher-invader and his preconceptions" (quoted in Vidal 9). This observation provides an insight into Flaherty's method, for what he recorded was not always what he found. In his nonfiction films, as Flaherty developed a slight narrative line to a simple but dramatic climax, he seldom let truth get in the way of a good story. Of this trait, Helen Van Dongen said:

> Some of the confusion arises because "documentary" is a confusing word, a catch-all for almost anything that is not straight fiction. To me Flaherty is *not* a documentarian; he makes it all up. He does use the documentary style and background but, except for *The Land,* they are all, to a degree, stories. He sets back the clock a hundred years if this suits him, so that living conditions, clothes (or no clothes) and weapons look more historic, not to say more romantic. Certainly the Eskimos at one time had to literally fight for survival, but by the time Flaherty came to Eskimo-land they already bought their guns *and* gramophones at the local trading post. I have no quarrel whatsoever with the way he makes his films. They are part of our history of filmmaking, but I do hesitate to call them documentaries. They are Flaherty-films, and worthwhile enjoying. (quoted in Achtenberg 51)

Flaherty believed that "a story must come out of the life of a people, not from the actions of individuals" (Rosenheimer 1–23); because he saw life as the struggle of man against nature, he did not look for the unique quality that sets Inuit apart from Aran Islanders or midwestern American farmers from Cajun bayou dwellers. Moving from one life to another, from one person to another, he sought what is inspiring in the lives of others, trusting that his audience would seek (and find) it with him. Insisting on integrity of vision, Flaherty rejected as spurious what Kracauer defined as the "semidocumentary," the fictional film that contains documentary foot-age: "You cannot superimpose studio-fabricated plots on an actual setting without finding that the reality of the background will show up the ar-tificiality of your story" (quoted in Goodman 3). However, Flaherty's own approach could be synthetic. For example, in *Elephant Boy* (a cinematic adaptation of a Rudyard Kipling story), Flaherty defended his method by rejecting the studio's script. However, the narrative that he created was a hybrid, neither Kipling nor Flaherty, neither fiction nor fact.

Siegfried Kracauer emphasizes Flaherty's reliance on the "found story" (245–49), what Paul Rotha calls Flaherty's "slight narrative." According to Kracauer, Flaherty took for granted that a narrative story would emerge from his approach: first, he found simple stories in the lives of people who lived close to nature, and then he created slight dramas of interest and suspense around certain heroes. Flaherty's dependence on the "found story" is also observed by John Grierson:

> Flaherty illustrates better than anyone the first principles of documentary. (1) It must master its material on the spot, and come in intimacy to ordering it. Flaherty digs himself in for a year, or two maybe. He lives with his people till the story is told "out of himself." (2) It must follow him in his distinction between description and drama. I think we shall find that there are other forms of drama, or more accurately, other forms of film than the one he chooses; but it is important to make the primary distinction between a method which describes only the surface value of a subject, and the method which more explosively reveals the reality of it. You photograph the natural life, but you also, by your juxtaposition of detail, create an interpretation of it. (*Grierson on Documentary* 148)

For Grierson, it is the shaping of reality through this juxtaposition of detail, the "interpretation of it," that separates the realist filmmaker from the artist who "describes only the surface value of the subject." It is what separates the complex *re*-presentation of reality found in the direct cinema approach, developed in the late 1950s and 1960s, from Flaherty's romantic approach to reality.

V

An artist of a strong and uniquely personal vision, Robert Flaherty made films that constitute their own genre. He was born a teller of tales, and like the ancient bards, he repeated essentially one story, embroidering it in each new telling with a different design. His was a simple, sublime design, achieved by the natural skills of a steadfast, independent artist who was caught early in the tangles of his own imagination. Hardly naive, he must to some extent have contributed to the image that gained currency—that of an idealistic, conservative, even reactionary, self-conscious, and astute artist.

CHAPTER TWO

Nanook of the North (1922)

"The aggie will come first"

I

Robert Flaherty had little formal education and apparently even less desire to obtain one. As a boy, he was interested in two things that stayed with him throughout his life—stories and music—and he enjoyed learning to play the violin and reading the works of authors who wrote about the West and the wilderness. His father, an explorer and mine manager, moved from one place to another throughout the greater Lake Superior region, sometimes without his wife and children, most often to mining communities where there was no school. In spite of these nomadic conditions, Flaherty's boyhood was pleasant. Education, however, became a matter of learning practical skills rather than developing intellectual ones. He did attend several schools for short periods, but, impatient with their lack of challenge and excitement, felt himself destined to be trained as an explorer, not as an artist, and to follow in his father's vocation.[10]

The life of an explorer was a hard, cold, dangerous, and unpredictable one, but determined men could find a region rich in minerals and unlimited opportunities for success. In 1896, when Flaherty was 12, his father accepted a position as manager of the Golden Star Mine near Rainy Lake, Ontario, just north of the Minnesota-Canada border; Flaherty went along and stayed almost two years. About 1898, at his mother's insistence, he went to Toronto and attended Upper Canada College, a preparatory school in the British tradition, but he was attracted more by the athletics program than the classroom, and shortly returned with his father to the frontier. They stayed in rough camps, with the traders and trappers, both white and Indian, and in this virtually unknown and sometimes hostile country, Flaherty learned the survival skills that mattered most: exploring, map making, prospecting, trapping animals, trading.

In 1900, when Flaherty was 16, the family moved to Port Arthur, Ontario, on the northern side of Lake Superior. Two years later, in a final, brief attempt at a formal education, Flaherty studied for seven months at the Michigan College of Mines in Houghton, Michigan, on the southern side of the lake. He was still not a conscientious student—indeed, he was expelled—but it was there that he met Frances Hubbard. He lacked formal education and had lived primarily on the borders of Lake Superior. She had had a college education, traveled in Europe, accompanied her father, a distinguished scientist, on geological explorations But, despite the differences in their backgrounds, they had much in common. They shared a love of nature and the wilderness, and spent a lifetime together traveling, studying, writing, and making photographs and films. In the fourteen years that elapsed before they were married, Flaherty undertook many trips in the Canadian wilderness, surveying for the railroads and exploring for minerals. In these further explorations, Flaherty deepened his love for the natural world that was to be the subject of his filmmaking career, a career that, symmetrically, began and ended with an exploration, first for iron ore *(Nanook of the North)* and last for oil *(Louisiana Story)*. Throughout, he seems never to have grown tired of observing nature and recording his impressions of man's relationship with it.

Next to his father, the man most responsible for Flaherty's subsequent development as an explorer and, almost ironically, as an artist, was Sir William Mackenzie, the Canadian railroad builder and financier, for whom the elder Flaherty worked as a consulting engineer. Young Flaherty had already made a name for himself as an explorer, and in 1910 Mackenzie commissioned him to explore the iron ore possibilities of the chain of islands outlying the sub-Arctic eastern coast of Hudson Bay. Flaherty enthusiastically accepted the challenge that he later described as "a turning point" in his life.[11] Between 1910 and 1912, under the most adverse conditions, he made two expeditions, traveling through ice and snow by foot and by canoe, keeping a diary, and making still photographs. Because he succeeded principally in improving the maps of the territory, rather than locating minerals, Flaherty was determined to return.[12] Agreeing to finance this third trip, Mackenzie provided *The Laddie,* a ship capable of icebreaking, as well as the equipment necessary for an eighteen-month expedition.

Flaherty's career as a filmmaker began before that trip started in August 1913. Although there are various versions of this story, Flaherty's own words best capture the spirit:

> Just as I was leaving, Sir William said to me casually, "Why don't you get one of these new-fangled things called a motion picture camera?" So I bought

one but with no other thought really than of taking notes on our exploration. We were going into interesting country, we'd see interesting people. I
had not thought of making a film for the theatres. I knew nothing whatsoever about films. (quoted in Rotha, ed. Ruby, 22)

Before setting out, however, he took three weeks to study camera operation and cinematography at the Eastman Company in Rochester, New
York. He had used a Kodak still camera on the first two expeditions, but as
far as anyone seems to know, this short course was to be his only formal
training in filmmaking, as his seven months at the Michigan College of
Mines was to be his only formal training in mineralogy.[13] Flaherty came to
love and use photography not only for exploration but for its own sake. His
first camera, a 1912 Bell and Howell, was sophisticated for the times and
ideal for studio work; but it proved unsuitable for use in the extreme Arctic
cold, for it was lubricated with an oil that thickened in the low temperatures
and had to be warmed between takes (Brownlow 473). Nevertheless, Flaherty loved to experiment and to discover for himself the potential of any
equipment. Orson Welles remarked: "He loved a gadget in a very American
way, as a thing in itself and not for what it could do" (quoted in Rotha, ed.
Ruby, 288). At the start of his career, Flaherty's enthusiasm was perhaps a
greater asset than technical knowledge or experience.

It was September 1913 when Flaherty finally set off for the sub-Arctic
again to work for Mackenzie—exploring, map making, and sampling minerals. He took his Bell and Howell camera, simple lighting equipment, and
portable developing and printing machine, but it was not until February
1914 that he found the time to use his new camera.[14] By October 1914, this
third expedition was completed, and even though he later concluded that
commercial mining in the area would not be practical or profitable, Flaherty considered it professionally successful and personally rewarding. For
his help in locating and mapping the Belcher Islands, the Canadian government subsequently named the largest of the islands after him.[15] More
important to his subsequent career, he had shot a certain amount of motion
picture film. After his return to New York, on 12 November 1914 he and
Frances Hubbard were married. During the 1914–15 winter, dodging his
wife's parents' attempts to persuade him to settle down—one of their plans
was that he would run a Ford automobile agency—he tried to put his film
into some kind of order. Although it proved too crude to be of much
interest, the amateur filmmaker wrote in *My Eskimo Friends* that he was
determined to make a better film on his next expedition (126).

Flaherty made his fourth and last expedition for Mackenzie in the summer of 1915, accompanied part of the way by his wife, his brother David, and

others. Again his principal activities were related to prospecting and map-making, but he also found time to shoot film showing the life, crafts, and customs of the people he encountered. From his journals, we learn that the Eskimos enjoyed being photographed and often vied for prominent places in front of the camera. This first encounter with the camera's effect on behavior taught him much about dealing with later subjects.

By the end of 1915, when Flaherty had completed the third and fourth expeditions for Mackenzie, he had shot approximately 70,000 feet (or 17 hours) of film. Returning to Toronto, and encouraged by his wife, he made a rough work print, known as the "Harvard Print"[16] because it was sent to Harvard University for a screening. Later, while packing the negative for shipment to New York, he carelessly dropped a lighted cigarette on the floor, where the scraps of flammable nitrate stock immediately went up in flames, seriously injuring Flaherty and destroying the rest of the negative as well. This potentially tragic accident proved to be a spur to his development as a filmmaker. Even though he could have made a duplicate negative from the work print and continued to work on this film, he did not choose to do so.[17] When he screened the positive "Harvard Print" for friends in New York, Flaherty realized that his audience was much less interested in the film than in the location in which it was made. As he later said:

> It was a bad film; it was dull—it was little more than a travelogue. I had learned to explore, I had not learned to reveal. It was utterly inept, simply a scene of this and that, no relation, no thread of a story or continuity whatever. . . . Certainly it bored me.[18]

At thirty-two, having established a successful career as an explorer, Flaherty concluded that such arduous work kept him away from home for too long at a time and that he did not want to continue it. Intrigued with filmmaking, encouraged by his wife, and determined to make a better film, Flaherty planned the making of what would become *Nanook of the North*.

II

The factual film had been born in 1895 in Paris when Auguste and Louis Lumière began to document everyday human activity; it was later developed by filmmakers who went along to document important expeditions on film. By 1908, "travelogue," the word coined by Burton Holmes, was being used to describe the short travel lectures with slides presented between reels at motion picture shows. These slides, the focus of Holmes' lectures, provided, in the words of Kevin Brownlow, "a sort of Baedeker of illuminated information" (420). Among these early travel filmmakers were Cherry Kearton, who filmed Theodore Roosevelt's 1909 African expedition; Herbert Ponting, whose film about Robert Falcon Scott's 1910–13 tragic expedition was released in 1913 as *The Undying Story of Captain Scott* and again in 1933 with sound as *Ninety Degrees South;* Emery and Ellsworth Kolb, who made films in the Grand Canyon in 1911; Martin Johnson, whose *Jack London in the South Seas* (1912) Flaherty admired; and Lowell Thomas, who in 1914 and again in 1915 shot footage in Alaska. These pioneers established the tradition which led to *Nanook of the North.* But, as Paul Rotha shows, Flaherty's work significantly differed from that of his predecessors.

> First, he combined the talents of a trained explorer and mineralogist with those of a filmmaker. He learned the technique of cinematography for himself, the hard way, in order to express what he himself found among the people on his expedition. Second, he was familiar with Eskimos and the land where they lived and where he was going to make his film, having eight years of experience among them. He knew his subject at first hand, a tenet that was to become an integral part of every Flaherty film. Third, and perhaps most important of all, his abortive first attempts at filming in 1913 and again in 1915 had shown him clearly that just to set up his camera and record scenes in a strange country was not sufficient to dramatize the struggle for survival of his friends, the Eskimos. Flaherty knew that something fundamental was lacking in his early efforts; he knew when he went north again in 1920 that it was not just to remake what he had lost in the flames at Toronto. (Rotha, ed. Ruby, 40)

Between 1916 and 1920, Flaherty tried hard to find a sponsor for his project, but most people during those years were too preoccupied with the World War I crisis to pay much attention, so the Flahertys used that time effectively to write and to begin their family.[19] In 1920, when he was thirty-six, he finally found a financial backer in John Revillon of Revillon Frères, the French furriers. For both Revillon Frères and Flaherty, it was an ideal relationship. Revillon had competed for years with the Hudson's Bay Company for domination of the fur business, so they regarded the film as a new and unique means for gaining both business and publicity. Flaherty had tried for four years to find financial support and now had a generous agreement that gave him substantial financial backing and artistic freedom.[20] Revillon's $53,000 budget included a $500 monthly salary for Flaherty for an unstipulated period, $13,000 for equipment and technical costs, and $3,000 credit at the Revillon trading post at Port Harrison for "remuneration of natives."[21]

For the first time, Flaherty went to the Arctic with the sole purpose of making a motion picture, reaching Port Harrison on the upper northeast Hudson Bay in August 1920. This time, however, he had acquired both practical filmmaking experience and suitable equipment. So that he could photograph in the extreme cold, he chose two Akeley cameras that were lubricated with graphite rather than oil or grease. He made another significant decision in choosing a gyro-head tripod, an important technical innovation that would enable him easily to pan or tilt the camera. While camera movement is not a vital stylistic element in *Nanook of the North,* the decision to use the gyro-head tripod was an innovation, for, as Rotha (ed. Ruby) points out, pans and tilts "are an important—indeed a vital—feature of all his subsequent work" (29). In addition to this relatively sophisticated and flexible camera equipment, he took equipment for developing, printing, and projecting his work (Murphy 7).

Flaherty made his first film in a way unique to him, in collaboration with the Eskimo subjects of the film, not, as has always been customary to the film industry, in collaboration with a crew. He hoped that the Inuit would accept and understand what he was doing and would work together with him as partners. The first sequence to be shot, the walrus hunt, would be a test of this working method, which Flaherty and Nanook discussed:

> "Suppose we go," said I, "do you know that you and your men may have to give up making a kill, if it interferes with my film? Will you remember that it is the picture of you hunting the iviuk [walrus] that I want and not their meat?"
>
> "Yes, yes, the aggie [motion picture] will come first," earnestly he assured me. "Not a man will stir, not a harpoon will be thrown until you give the sign. It is my word."
>
> We shook hands and agreed to start the next day.[22]

This agreement secured the natives' cooperation, provided technical assistance, and, perhaps most important, helped to ensure that the film would present their point of view. For sixteen months, Flaherty and the Eskimos lived, worked, and suffered as equal partners (Rotha, ed. Ruby, 36). Of this unique collaboration, Andrew Sarris observed:

> One of the most beautiful moments in the history of the cinema was recorded when Nanook smilingly acknowledged the presence of Flaherty's camera in his igloo. The director was not spying on Nanook or attempting to capture Nanook's life in the raw. He was collaborating with Nanook on a representation rather than a simulation of existence. What Flaherty understood so well was the potential degeneration of the documentary into voyeurism when the images of the camera were not reprocessed in the mind of the artist. (42–43)

Flaherty with an Inuit woman outside an igloo in the Arctic.

Although Sarris acknowledges that their collaboration prevented voyeurism, he overlooks the fact that it also obligated Nanook to help Flaherty create a view of Eskimo life that was both representation and simulation.

Because he was paying the Eskimos for their work, Flaherty had at least a commercial right to demand that his work take priority over theirs. But there was no conflict of interest for the Eskimos, for Nanook and his friends already had rifles, and thus no real need for harpoons, and the thought of losing a walrus must not have worried them. There is no question that theirs was a life of struggle for food, shelter, existence—Nanook died two years later of starvation on a hunting trip; nevertheless, their willingness to help in creating a work of art that deals with elemental facts of life, not their own immediate needs, also implies that the Eskimos knew the difference between art and life. For Flaherty, having their cooperation in delineating the difference between reality and film was a major step in bringing him closer to becoming an artist.

The Eskimos taught Flaherty that art is more than just an expression of life's values, that it enables man to understand his relationship to life, and that it is also artifact, a utilitarian record of the moment.[23] The Eskimo sees life clearly and simply, in terms of existence and action, and his art affirms his conquest of his hostile environment. In carvings, he reveals a form that makes a statement against the formlessness of his environment. The Eskimo's approach is to explore, conquer, and record. For Flaherty, too, filmmaking was an act of exploration first and affirmation second. Later, in editing *Nanook,* Flaherty took into account the aesthetics of Eskimo art, as well as those of the fiction, travel, and adventure films of the day. Most important of these are the influence of Eskimo art and the rhythm of Eskimo life, especially in the conception and narrative structure of *Nanook.*

Flaherty said that "a story must come out of the life of a people, not from the actions of individuals" (quoted in Rosenheimer 9). For him, the natural world—a generalized society—was much easier than the human, individualized world to present on the screen because it did not require the portrayal of human conversation or the conflict that comes from human interaction. In *Nanook,* he showed primitive man's realization that his destiny lay in his own hands, that it was his obligation to improve his lot on earth by working, and that the members of his family were probably his first and most important helpers. In concentrating on the life of Nanook and his family (which was, theoretically and practically "extended" to include Flaherty himself), Flaherty chose a theme that Sigmund Freud maintained was one of the foundations of civilization:

> The communal life of human beings had, therefore, a two-fold foundation: the compulsion to work, which was created by external necessity, and the power to love, which made the man unwilling to be deprived of his sexual object—the woman—and made the woman unwilling to be deprived of the part of herself which had been separated off from her—her child. Eros and Anake [love and necessity] have become the parents of human civilization too. (48)

Flaherty's respect for this communal life, this oneness with nature, is reflected in the narrative of the film. As Siegfried Kracauer says, the film-maker's "creativity manifests itself in letting nature in and penetrating it" (40). A brief synopsis of *Nanook* follows.[24]

III

Nanook of the North, which originally carried with it one of two possible subtitles—either *A Story of Life and Love in the Actual Arctic* or *A Story of the Snowlands*—begins with an intertitle: "No other race could survive . . . yet here live the most cheerful people in all the world—the fearless, lovable, happy-go-lucky Eskimos." An orientation map shows the Ungava Penin-sula on the eastern shore of Hudson Bay. Close-up shots introduce the film's principal characters: Nanook (played by an Inuit named Allaka-riallak) and his wife Nyla. Later, in a scene that reminds viewers of a comic device used to introduce clowns in a circus, the whole family is intro-duced, each member emerging after the other from a kayak that does not appear large enough to hold them all. This also introduces their closeness as a family, which, when they all sleep together, has the practical advantage of permitting them to share body heat. Next we see how the Eskimos use moss for fuel and how they make and repair their kayaks, practical activities that were always of interest to Flaherty in his later films.

The second sequence records the annual journey in which Nanook and his family carry their boat over land to the river and then paddle it to the fur company's trading post. Nanook displays skins, furs, and his husky pup-pies, while his wife Nyla displays their infant Rainbow. Both the dogs and children are important symbols in the film. Nanook is so fascinated by the trader's phonograph record that he tries to bite a record, an amusing bit of theatrical business that loses credibility in the face of the fact that Flaherty had consistently kept Nanook and his friends amused and entertained with his own phonograph. The children are treated to sea biscuits and lard, but their overindulgence necessitates castor oil, which for them is also a treat.

In the brief third sequence, Nanook shows his skill as a fisherman. Using bits of ivory tusk as bait on a seal-string line, he fishes through a hole in the ice, spearing the fish that rise to the bait near the surface. This is followed by a major sequence of walrus hunting, in which Flaherty effectively relates the suspense of the hunt to the hunger of the family. Nanook and other hunters respond in a fleet of kayaks to news that a herd of walrus has been sighted on a nearby shore. In a tug-of-war, they harpoon one of these great beasts, drag it to shore, and eat raw some of its meat. Here, as in the shark hunting scenes in *Man of Aran,* men had to learn and use outdated methods, but unlike the seal hunting scene later in *Nanook,* the walrus sequence has not been staged.

The fifth sequence is concerned with a winter storm, yet another element with which the Eskimos must struggle for survival. While Nanook and his family are evidently still (or again) at the trading post, which is almost completely obliterated by the snow, they embark on a hunting trip. The continuity is confused by the unclear chronology and the unmatched shots. The dog team drags the sledge over difficult, icy terrain. Nanook retrieves a white fox, still alive, from one of his traps. Nightfall brings the necessity for shelter. With the assurance and skill of an engineer and fine craftsman, Nanook cuts blocks of frozen snow and fits them together to make an igloo, finishing by inserting a block of clear ice into the structure to make a window.[25] His control over nature seems so masterful that one wonders how survival could ever be a problem. Next he teaches his young son how to shoot a toy bow and arrow. This tender sequence reinforces three interlocked themes: the family's closeness, the necessity of one generation's passing on its skills to the next, and survival as a matter of both skill and tradition. The family settles in for the long night.

At the beginning of the final sequence, they awaken to the usual morning activities. Nyla chews Nanook's boots to soften the leather and then washes the baby with her saliva. Nanook uses his saliva to glaze the runners of the sledge, but before they depart on the journey, the hungry dogs ominously begin to fight among themselves. Once underway, Nanook searches for food. He finds a breathing hole in the ice and through it spears a seal. There are Chaplinesque overtones in this long, comic struggle between Nanook and the seal under the ice.[26] We do not know what is struggling on the other end of the line, what makes Nanook exert so much energy, until the seal is finally hauled out onto the ice. It was clearly dead before Nanook began the struggle, and Flaherty's obvious fakery can be explained by one of his best known remarks: "Sometimes you have to lie. One often has to distort a thing to catch its true spirit."[27] In his tug-of-war with the seal, Nanook loses his balance and falls head over heels, much to the amusement of other members of the family. But there is a serious side to all of this, too, for all the people and the dogs are hungry. While they butcher the seal and enjoy some raw meat, the dogs fight so viciously over the scraps that are thrown to them that they tangle their lines and dangerously delay the continuation of the journey back to the camp.

Flaherty creates suspense by showing the day coming to an end, with the dogs getting hungrier and more violent, the weather getting nastier, and the family being forced to take shelter in an abandoned igloo. However, they sleep warmly as the storm outside turns the landscape into a white fury. The film ends in an unresolved scene with tragic implications. The family is lost, the dogs are shown sleeping under a heavy blanket of snow, and there is no suggestion of what morning will bring. However, if the film to this point has not suggested that these people have the strength to get through such a night, then no ending (actual or staged) would convey it. It is the most perfect moment in any Flaherty film, full of the rich ambiguity of meaning inherent in human life.

IV

In this narrative, Flaherty's self-stated goal was to show the Eskimos' "former majesty and character." By staging some scenes, inventing others, and omitting the white man almost entirely (except for a brief shot at the trading post), Flaherty keeps our attention on this theme. Although the imposed fictional narrative diminishes the film's value as a factual record, it does give it structure, lends it charm, and emphasizes human character.[28] The noble picture that emerges of Nanook is but one result of his relationship with Flaherty. The filmmaker and his subject were admirably suited to one another, not as master and material, but as men who understood and respected one another. Both were individualists, craftsmen, and artists; both had a sense of humor; both approached the elements of their respective lives with gentleness, warmth, and affection. Nanook, more than the master of his environment, is the master of himself, a hero who endures and prevails and who, without pride, has the humility of a man who wages a life and death struggle with nature each day.

The power and charm of the film come not only from Nanook and his way of life, but also from Flaherty's respect for that life, which prevented him from exploiting Nanook or over-emphasizing the hardship and severity of his life for theatrical purposes.[29] The adversity seen in the film is Nanook's, and it belongs to his culture, not ours. He has never known enough warmth to know how bitterly cold his world is to us. It is we who suffer by empathy and by the knowledge of how much one man will give in order that he and his family might live. The conflict here is between man and nature, with the final shots confirming its unpredictable resolution. Flaherty is true to the rhythm of life by refusing to force that rhythm into some preconceived ending. The film ends where it began—with Nanook and his family in what we can accept as a reasonably reliable account of their life.

However, *Nanook of the North* raises for the first time an issue that is pertinent to the discussion of any Flaherty film: whether or not it can be considered as a truthful document. In reaching some conclusion on this issue, Flaherty's stated intentions for the film (and the statements are not consistent) must be considered along with other factors relevant to the film's production. *Nanook* is true to human nature, but not true to the life that the Eskimos were living when Flaherty made the film. It does not have either the wholly fictional narrative of a theatrical film or the factual reliability of an ethnographic film. For example, Rotha (ed. Ruby) writes: "No reference is made to social practices such as the sexual life or marriage customs of the Eskimo, so the film has little real anthropological value" (39). As a work of art, not of social science, the film's value is its truth to the basic needs of man and the essential rhythms of life, its illumination of man's industry, capacity for love, and potential for nobility.

V

Nanook of the North was the first effort of a man whose experience lay in shooting, not shaping, motion picture footage, a man who knew less about filmmaking than most beginning film production students know today; nonetheless, its achievements are remarkable. His handling of cinematic time and space increases our involvement with Nanook and his family, centering our interest on the actual event, rather than on its dramatic significance or meaning. For example, when Nanook is struggling with the seal, a simulated scene, Flaherty preserves the actual length of waiting time in unedited footage, and he respects spatial unity by encompassing the entire action in one shot.[30] How far Flaherty went from his apparent respect for the conventions of realism to those of formalism can be seen by contrasting the attitudes that characterize his first and last films. In *Louisiana Story,* his last film, he exploits the dramatic possibilities of the alligator fight (also a simulation); through Helen Van Dongen's shot/reverse shot montage, and the music that accompanies it, we imagine all the dangers of an event that we never really see on the screen.

As a filmmaker, Flaherty's strengths are in his narrative imagination, rather than in his handling of the cinematic form that expresses it. He recognized form in nature, and took great care and attention in photographing his subject, but sometimes overlooked the formal elements within the subject that would enable him to relate it to his larger purpose. From *Nanook* on, his method was to immerse himself in the subject, to shoot everything with the hope of capturing cinematographic images that

An Inuit drawing of Flaherty photographing the igloo-
building scene; note the depiction of three cameras.

would preserve the temporal and spatial realities of what his observant eyes
perceived. Although this would appear to be the ideal method of discovering a subject, of letting it unfold and reveal itself, it contributed to the lack
of purpose often evident in his subsequent films. His intuitive approach
made it almost impossible for editors to deal with his footage along the
principles traditionally associated with editing.[31] When he began working
with Helen Van Dongen in 1940, he began to discover the alternative
approach whereby cinematic form is achieved through a collaborative
process that begins with the filmmaker's imagination of how the film will
look and move, continues with the cinematographer's translation of that
idea into footage, and ends with the editor's shaping of that footage to
meet, as nearly as possible, the filmmaker's original conception. But even
late in his career, he found it difficult to reconcile this process with his
intuitive approach to filmmaking.

Although *Nanook* shows Flaherty's mastery of some aspects of film grammar, it also shows him struggling with some problems that other contemporary filmmakers had already solved. Among the problems evident in the
film are static tableaux; lack of establishment shots, for which intertitles
attempt to compensate; awkward tilting and panning, hardly necessary
with the gyro-head tripod he was using; and other problems in visual

continuity and style.[32] However, with his technique (deep-focus lenses, long takes, re-framing), he achieved a high degree of cinematic realism within individual shots, scenes, or sequences. He could maintain narrative continuity through constant screen direction (the direction in which characters move from shot to shot), as, for example, in the final sequence when Nanook and his family seek shelter. He used rudimentary parallel editing to retain narrative continuity, as when the "while father works" title card is followed by shots of children playing, or to reinforce the motif of hunger, when the seal is being butchered and cross-cuts show the snarling dogs. He also used this simple parallel editing to heighten suspense. Rotha (ed. Ruby) has remarked that suspense—keeping the audience guessing and revealing the secret only at the last moment—became a significant aspect of his narrative style in later films (38). Flaherty used dissolves in the traditional way, to show the passing of time. He had a nice sense of the visual joke, as when the family emerge from their kayak, and a good mastery of suspense, as when Nanook fights the seal. And he used symbols effectively, particularly the dogs as representative of the Eskimos' isolation, loneliness, and stubborn instinct for survival.

Another strength is Flaherty's overall use of these elements in a silent film. Even though the technology for making a synchronized sound film was not available in 1920, Flaherty knew how much natural sounds might have contributed to *Nanook:* "I wish I could have had sound for *Nanook.* . . . It takes the hiss of the wind in the North and the howls of the dogs to get the whole feeling of that country" (quoted in Kracauer 128). The producers of both the 1947 and the 1976 re-releases of the film have taken this rather too literally, for the sound effects and musical scores in these versions do not so much simulate sounds that approximate what we see on the screen as recall the efforts of theatre pianists and organists to create atmosphere for silent films.[33] While Flaherty's cinematic sensibility was almost wholly limited to creating visual images, he understood the role that sound plays in our perception of reality but did not master the integration of visual and aural images until the end of his career.

VI

Like many independent filmmakers before and since, Flaherty had a difficult time in securing distribution for *Nanook.* Major American distributors rejected it, but eventually Pathé released it on 11 June 1922 at New York City's Capitol Theater on a bill with *My Country,* the third of Robert C. Bruce's "Wilderness Tales."[34] Both films were held over for a second week, and *Nanook* was subsequently sold for national and international distribution and was promoted as a major release.[35] By September 1926, four years later, Flaherty reported that its worldwide gross receipts were $251,000, yielding a profit to himself and Revillon Frères of $36,000, of which Flaherty received half (Barnouw, "Robert Flaherty (Barnouw's File)" 165). Revillon continued to profit indirectly from the association of its name with *Nanook of the North,* Nanook's name was given to a German ice-cream bar, the "Nanuk," and celebrated in an American popular song,[36] and of all Flaherty's films, it is the one most associated with his name by the general motion picture audience and critics alike.

Nanook's status as a "classic" in the history of cinema is largely unquestioned. It remains unique in its interweaving of dramatic story with what appeared to be actual life, and critics praised its originality, charm, tenderness, educational value, and what they believed to be its truth.[37] European critics were, if anything, even more enthusiastic than their American counterparts. It is true that, in 1926, Iris Barry, who was to become the Director of the Department of Film of the Museum of Modern Art and a voice in the development of the American nonfiction film, questioned the authenticity of the film's portrayal of Eskimo life.[38] While some critics still continue to make such judgments, they are few in contrast to those who understand Flaherty's methods, as well as his strengths and weaknesses, and evaluate his films accordingly.

Nanook is a simple film about an ordinary man who survives in circumstances that are ordinary to him, but which seem extraordinary to us. Flaherty discovered and revealed Nanook's way of life through his acute observation, lack of condescension, intimate presentation of detail, and determination to allow the material to shape its own meaning. However, his attempts to sell the film and his apparent acquiescence to its vulgar commercial promotion indicate that from the start Flaherty actively sought to make his mark in the commercial motion picture industry. This theatrical yearning was present from the beginning and proved to be an obstacle in his later efforts to preserve the integrity of his approach. It is not known what gains as a filmmaker Flaherty might have made from analyzing the strengths and weaknesses of *Nanook* or from studying the work of his contemporaries, who, like him, were pioneers in the development of cinematic form and language. But he does not appear to have made such an analysis of *Nanook,* probably because he was proud of *Nanook's* success and eager to begin *Moana: A Romance of the Golden Age,* with its opportunity to work with panchromatic film stock and long focus lenses. Two conclusions appear certain: there was an audience for factual films (even those with fictional narrative and deliberate re-staging), and these films could be a box-office success.

In pure approach and simple achievement, *Nanook of the North* was the zenith of Flaherty's career. He never sought again to immerse himself in a foreign culture in anything like the way he did in the Arctic, a way that, despite its physical and psychological pressures, seems in retrospect to have been essential to his success. He never again allowed his subject to reveal itself as fully, but rather went out with a preconception to discover the one thing for which he was looking, and then to alter actuality to fit his vision of what it should be. He once said: "There is a saying among prospectors—'Go out looking for one thing, that's all you'll ever find'" (quoted in Rotha and Wright, "Nanook of the North" 33). For the rest of his career after *Nanook*, he sought many things—among them independence, a place in the motion picture industry, and fame—but he never again looked for them with the clarity of purpose, innocence, and wonder of discovery that led him to make his first film. And he never again made a film that was so clearly expressive of his instincts as an explorer and an artist.

CHAPTER THREE

Moana: A Romance of the Golden Age (1926)

The Perils of Beauty

I

In February 1923, nine months after *Nanook of the North* was released, Robert Flaherty received an offer to make his second film for Jesse Lasky, head of Famous Players-Lasky, the production division of Paramount Pictures.[39] Flaherty was enjoying *Nanook*'s critical and commercial success, and this offer, which represented the first important turning point in his career, confirmed his public recognition as a professional filmmaker. Fascinated by exploration, Lasky made an offer that was irresistible to Flaherty—to go anywhere in the world to make a film of exploration—but he added the condition that it should be another *Nanook* (Murphy 11). Both Flaherty and his wife were concerned about maintaining a stable life for their family, and realized that a new film project would take Flaherty away from home and from his responsibilities as husband and father for another long period. Rather than choose between his career and his family, Flaherty determined that making films did not preclude traveling with his family, and he decided to sign a contract with Lasky. While this decision established the pattern of family living that remained successful throughout his life, it had a less positive effect on his career as a filmmaker.[40]

Although Flaherty did not yet know where he wanted to make his second film, he had decided that it would be in an indigenous culture where the integrity of native life was threatened by outside cultural influence (Murphy 11). Convinced by friends that he should seek out and record a Polynesian culture, Flaherty chose the Samoan Islands in the South Seas as the site.[41] At this point in his career, Samoa offered many advantages. The island had an allure as unusual and as exotic as that of the Arctic; it offered

Flaherty an opportunity to record another culture undergoing rapid change; and its temperate climate made the island attractive for his wife and children. Lasky would provide a budget sufficient for making the film as well as for Flaherty's experimentation with cameras, lenses, and film stock. And, of course, it offered the opportunity for travel half way around the world.

In April 1923, Flaherty—accompanied by his wife, their three daughters, his younger brother, David, and the children's nursemaid—arrived in the village of Safune on the Samoan island of Savaii, which was to be their home until their return to the United States in December 1924. Flaherty also took sixteen tons of filmmaking equipment, including, for black and white work, the Akeley camera with a gyro-head tripod he used on *Nanook*, a developing laboratory, and an electric generating plant. Since he planned to experiment with the new panchromatic film stock, he also took a Prizma color camera.

While Flaherty's decision to travel and work together with his family provided him with companionship, it also meant that he would have to adapt his singular ways to a new working arrangement. In making *Moana*, according to Rotha (ed. Ruby), "Flaherty was the combined director-photographer; David and Frances Flaherty helped him organize, gave ideas, and made the wheels of production turn smoothly" (77). David Flaherty, his younger brother, who helped in the early stages of *Nanook*, was initially attracted to Samoa by the climate rather than by filmmaking, but he eventually became a filmmaker and continued, throughout his brother's lifetime, to play a part in Robert Flaherty's career. Frances Flaherty was an active woman, curious about the world around her, with interests in travel, exploration, and photography, as well as in her husband's work, and so she went along to Samoa, not only as wife and mother, but also as collaborator.[42] She had no direct experience in filmmaking, outside of her observation of the post-production period of *Nanook*, yet she wrote from the beginning of the Samoan adventure as if she and Robert Flaherty had long been a filmmaking team.

> This time we were making a film for Hollywood and we were very conscious of that fact. Bob had no illusions whatever as to what Paramount expected of him in the way of thrills and sensations for the box office. All the way down on the steamer we talked about it, conjured up this scene and that scene, imagining the sea monsters we might find lurking in the deep-sea caverns under the coral reefs that fringe the islands. When one day a report came in from another ship at sea that one of these monsters had been sighted—a giant octopus, its tentacles spread over the waters from a body the size of a whale—we were sure that we were on the right track. *(Odyssey* 19–20)

These preconceptions about what they might find in Samoa were shattered by their subsequent experiences.

During the three years that Flaherty was occupied with the *Moana* project, obstacles both major and minor prevented him from fully achieving his goals.[43] The problems included primitive living conditions, occasional strife among the natives, and his own mysterious illness.[44] One major difficulty was that Flaherty did not know the South Seas environment. He had explored the Arctic extensively before making *Nanook,* but before going to Samoa he knew only what he had read and heard about the South Seas, and arrived there as a filmmaker, not as an explorer. However, the most difficult obstacle to overcome was not too little familiarity with the geography or the culture, but too much fantasy. Frances Flaherty said:

> Our big idea was that we should make a film after the pattern of *Nanook of the North.* We should find a man like Nanook the Eskimo, a sturdy, dignified chief and head of a family, and then build our picture round him, substituting the dangers of the sea, here in the South Pacific, for those of snow and ice in the North. We would present the drama of Samoan life as it unrolled itself naturally before us, as far as possible untouched by the hand of the missionary and the government. We began by trying to tell the Polynesians in a booklet about the Eskimos and the purpose behind filming *Nanook.* (quoted in Griffith, *World* 54)

When they realized that their theme could not be the struggle with nature, Frances Flaherty recalled in "The Camera's Eye" that they found a different approach:

> For so many generations have they been practicing these beautiful movements that beauty has entered into even the commonest things they do, whether they sit or stand or walk or swim, there is that beauty of movement, rhythm, the philosophy, the story of their life. So that simply in the beautiful movement of a hand the whole story of that race can be revealed. Now we had the secret. Here was the matter for our philosophical camera's eye. We unpacked our cameras again. (346)

However, this approach also proved unsuccessful, and beautiful movement did not become a significant theme in *Moana.* More time elapsed as they searched again for the "secret" to making *Moana:* observation, not preconception.

During the early 1920s, pioneers in the field of anthropology were experiencing problems similar to those that Flaherty had had in the Arctic and was having again in Samoa. Like these anthropologists, Flaherty sought to achieve a non-ethnocentric depiction of an alien cultural tradition and thus to satisfy the ethnographer's goal, as defined by Bronislaw Malinowski, of grasping "the native's point of view, his relation to life, to realize his vision of the world."[45] Ethnography, which aims at understanding an environment on its own terms, is not an evaluative field of research. The term, "as used by anthropologists, means an analytic description of a culture which is the result of a long-term intensive period of participant/observation field research by a trained anthropologist" (Ruby 71). The ethnographer defers judgment, bringing theories of cultural relativism to bear on lengthy observations of a society in order to describe and interpret how it works. Quantitative researchers construct their hypotheses, constantly testing and refining them within a living and changing situation, observing and recording the dynamics of human processes in action. Qualitative researchers work on the site, observing the immediate and concrete human interactions of the social setting under investigation and interviewing participants in order to learn how they perceive critical incidents that have arisen. The ethnographic film—part science, part art—might be defined as the interaction of quantitative and qualitative methodologies.

Margaret Mead, whose first book, *Coming of Age in Samoa,* was published in 1928, two years after *Moana* was released, pioneered with Gregory Bateson the use of motion picture and still photography in ethnographic studies. The following excerpt from a discussion between them illustrates a continuing concern over the amount of invention and restructuring permissible in a film that purports to be factual.

> *Bateson:* Because I think a photographic record should be an art form.
> *Mead:* Oh why? Why shouldn't you have some records that aren't art forms? Because if it's an art form it has been altered.
> *Bateson:* It's undoubtedly been altered. I don't think it exists unaltered.
> *Mead:* I think it's very important, if you're going to be scientific about behavior to give other people access to the materials, as comparable as possible to the access you had. You don't, then, alter the material. There's a bunch of filmmakers now that are saying, "It should be art" and wrecking everything that we're trying to do. Why the hell should it be art? (Mead and Bateson 78)

This conversation illuminates one issue raised by a film such as *Moana:* the degree of manipulation either inherent or allowable in a film record of a living culture. Flaherty's familiar dictum that a filmmaker "often has to distort a thing to catch its true spirit" raises major concerns for the ethnographer, both at the structural and behavioral levels. Certainly, in his quandary over how to make *Moana,* Flaherty seemed less concerned with preserving the materials he encountered than with creating art and entertainment.

Nor was the culture whose spirit Flaherty set out to capture as straightforward as he imagined it would be. As Murphy observes, the Flahertys "did not understand that what appears outwardly as a simple, primitive society, can be just as complicated and ritualistic with similar demands and anxieties as any modern day civilization" (12). At that time, the Samoans themselves were having difficulty in adjusting to the changes brought to their island by the passing of time, the British colonial government, and the Christian missionaries. Nevertheless, after several months devoted mainly to photographic experimentation, the Flahertys went forward with their plan to include within the film some customs that had almost disappeared, ignore many contemporary social problems, and generally alter Samoan life to fit the narrative that they imposed upon it. Felix David, the German trader who was the self-styled King of Savaii, complained that the alterations would misrepresent Samoan society, but not even this dissuaded the Flahertys. Added to the natives' concerns were Flaherty's cinematic requirements that they wear clothing that had long since been replaced by Western dress, affect longer hairstyles than those in fashion, and submit one of their young men to the almost defunct ritual of tattooing. Hardly deterred by opposition, Flaherty shot 240,000 feet of film, an astonishing amount even considering his almost unlimited supply of film stock. Following is a brief synopsis of what he created.

II

Moana, set on the Samoan island of Savaii, has as its principal characters Moana (the Samoan word for sea); Leupenga, his older brother; Pe'a, his younger brother; Tu'ungaita, his mother; Fa'angase, his fiancée; and old Tufunga, the tattooer. The episodic narrative moves through seven basic sequences that reveal Flaherty's characteristic fascination with what people do and how they make things, and also record the elaborate celebration and painful ritual through which Moana proves his claim to the Samoan tradition.

Flaherty begins *Moana* with a lyrical sequence that establishes two dominant motifs: a happy people and an abundant environment. Moana, a teenager, wears a sarong around his waist and a wreath of flowers in his hair. Dressed similarly is his bare-breasted fiancée, Fa'angase, who, a title card says, is "the loveliest maiden in the village." They are in the jungle gathering taro root, bananas, mulberry bark, and leaves; the leaves will be used for various household chores, such as wrapping food that is to be cooked for the feast, and the bark will be used for making cloth. Nearby

Moana (right) and his two brothers, Pe'a (center) and
Leupenga (left), in a Samoan outrigger canoe.

Tu'ungaita, Moana's mother, looks for her younger son, Pe'a, who is
playing under the trees. They are joined by others, and on the way home,
Moana lays a snare trap for the wild boar, "the one dangerous animal" on
the island. Flaherty shows this process in close-up detail, and another title
card informs us that the boar's tusks have killed "more than one Safune
man." Moana cuts a vine containing water and playfully gives his mother a
drink before they continue the downhill walk to Safune, their village by the
sea.

The second sequence begins with shots of the sea, the lagoon, and the
large village. A title card asks: "Meanwhile, what has happened at the
snare?" Moana and his two brothers return to the snare they set in the
jungle and find a boar trapped by the leg. After some struggle with the
vicious beast, cross-cut with shots of little Pe'a talking to his brothers from
the safety of a tree, they subdue the animal, tie it to a pole, and return to the
village. This activity and the previous food-gathering are all in preparation
for the ritual surrounding Moana's tattooing, but we are not told this until
just before the event is to take place. All other activities before that moment
are understood as taking place on one day.

Flaherty introduces another dominant motif in the third sequence: the bountiful sea. Moana and his brothers set out in an outrigger canoe to spear fish in the shallow, clear water of a lagoon protected by reefs. As it is depicted, fishing seems more like play than work. Along the shore, Fa'angase is gathering palm fronds and finds a "giant clam" (about the size of a basketball). Eventually, they all return to the village with more food for the feast.

Moana's fourth sequence provides a full account of the process through which Tu'ungaita, Moana's mother, makes cloth for a dress. Flaherty shows this in detail, obviously enjoying and respecting the simple methods. Tu'ungaita strips the mulberry bark, pounding and separating layer after layer until it becomes a kind of cloth; her helper crushes red seeds of sandalwood to make a dye, and then, following a pattern of her own design, Tu'ungaita fashions the typical Samoan skirt known as a lava-lava. Meanwhile, in search of coconuts, Moana and Pe'a sail to a nearby beach. With the aid of a rope hitch between his ankles, Pe'a climbs to the top of a towering coconut tree, twists the coconuts off and drops them down to Moana, who husks them on a sharp stick driven into the sand. Pe'a seems to be having a good time, scaling such a dangerous height, and like Mikeleen in *Man of Aran* sitting calmly on the edge of a sheer cliff, he seems content to be doing what is normal, what the filmmaker asks, or both.

Once again, in the fifth sequence, Moana and his brothers return to sea in their outrigger canoe. The big storm out at sea, evident throughout this scene, is balanced by a rainbow in the middle distance. The waves break over the reef into the lagoon, creating high waves that spume through a distant blowhole. They paddle through the waves, which overturn their canoe, but they safely return to shore, where they try to fish in a surf that is so rough that it knocks them against the rocks. Pe'a makes a fire by rubbing two sticks together and smokes a giant crab out of its hiding place. Moana spots a giant turtle (apparently all the animals in Samoa are huge) and wrestles it with his bare hands, and after a hard struggle, succeeds in getting the live reptile into the canoe. It is obviously a docile creature unwilling to put up much of a fight. Leupenga drills a hole in the turtle's shell and secures it with twine so that it can stay in the water but not escape. We are told that the tortoise shell is used for the islanders' most prized ornaments, but it is not clear if it will be the animal's fate to become part of the forthcoming feast. Meanwhile, Fa'angase flirts with Moana, teasing him with the small live fishes she is eating, "wiggle and all" (title card). Back in the village, Moana's mother and brothers get ready for the feast, preparing coconut milk custard, wrapping fish in leaves, and placing these things, along with bananas, breadfruit, and taro root, over heated stones to cook.

In the penultimate sequence, at the end of what is supposed to be one day, Fa'angase puts a flower in Moana's hair, ties tinkling shells around his ankles, and anoints him with perfumed oil. Together they perform the *siva* dance which, as a title tells us, prepares Moana for the "great event" of the tattooing that will signify his manhood. Flaherty keeps the camera almost exclusively on the handsome young man. The mutual eroticism inherent in this dance, so obviously sexual in gesture, is not developed in the film.

In the tattooing scene, old Tufunga works with sharp needles of bone, which are tapped into Moana's flesh, along with dyes, to make a permanent pattern. He is assisted by Moana's older brother, Leupenga, his mother, and his father, who is seen here for the first time in the film. All three men are tattooed. Moana's mother wipes the sweat from his brow and fans him, while his brother wipes the dye and blood from his body. His father and Fa'angase are passive observers. Although he filmed the entire process, Flaherty includes only footage of Moana's back and knees actually being marked. Later evidence of Moana's tattooed buttocks, and of lines running from his backside around his waist, suggests a greater overall coverage. We are told that the tattooing of the knee is the "hardest of all to bear,"[46] and Flaherty provides a title: "The deepest wisdom of the race has said that manhood shall be won through pain."

During the tattooing, Flaherty cuts to shots of a woman (the title reads: "Light your oven, witch-woman, Tufunga needs more dye") and then to shots of a large company of men performing a ritual dance outside the hut ("Courage to Moana!"). Since Flaherty has condensed six weeks of tattooing into a few minutes of film, we must accept this convention of cross-cutting and suspend all disbelief. Leupenga and Fa'angase make *kava,* a mixture of powdered root and water. After drinking some of this libation from a coconut shell, Tufunga, the tattoo artist, passes it to Moana's father. Later, inside the hut of Moana's parents, Leupenga is in a prayerful trance while his mother caresses the sleeping Pe'a. Outside, Moana and Fa'angase, with elaborate plumes in their hair, again dance the *siva,* this time in a rather more suggestive sexual frenzy. A title summarizes Moana's position in the world: "Prestige from his village, honor for his family, the maiden of his desire." *Moana* ends with a final slow pan shot of the village and surrounding countryside.

III

Moana: A Romance of the Golden Age is a fictitious idyll of Samoan life, as Flaherty intended. The term "golden age" in the subtitle, an allusion to an earlier, prosperous period during which man lived in ideal happiness, signifies that Flaherty is taking us to a time and place that are not of this world, yet the realistic day-in-the-life narrative structure tempts one to believe that the film provides an actual account of Samoan life. This structure is convenient, but it provides little opportunity to explain the background of what is being depicted. Still, Flaherty is more concerned here with natural beauty and human goodness than social commentary.

Moana follows the pattern established in *Nanook* and continued in later films: the introduction of a family followed by a record of its daily life. Unlike *Nanook,* the focus here is not on the father, but on Moana, the second of three sons, and on the preparations for his coming of age ritual. This family, unlike Nanook's, is not an actual one, but rather—as in *Man of Aran, Elephant Boy,* and *Louisiana Story*—one whose members were chosen from the larger community primarily for their attractiveness and willingness to "act" in a motion picture.

While *Moana* lulls audiences with the blissful life that its narrative portrays,[47] its narrative form raises questions about the director's alteration of fact. Although the Flahertys both maintained that the man-nature conflict was not relevant to a depiction of Samoan life, there were, in fact, many real dangers in the Samoan's world, only a few of which the film includes. Instead, as he did in *Nanook* and *Man of Aran,* Flaherty adds to the perceived danger by risking lives (young Pe'a's, for instance) to record dramatic footage in the midst of an impending storm at sea. And he submitted Ta'avale (Moana) to a physical disfigurement; although Flaherty paid Ta'avale for enduring the pain, the elaborate tattoos must have made more difficult his inevitable absorption into the Westernized culture. For the most part, however, *Moana* depicts a world in which danger is neutralized; for example, a sequence showing rough seas (prefiguring a motif of *Man of Aran*) concludes with a shot of a rainbow. What *Moana* offers us is a theatrical drama of Samoan life set in an unfamiliar world in which there is no significant form of adversity, either natural or human.

Another instance of Flaherty's inability to grasp, understand, and express the truth of Samoan life is evidenced by the inconsistencies connected with the tattooing scene. Before the tattooing is shown, a title informs us that "there is a rite through which every Polynesian must pass to win the right to call himself a man," but Ta'avale, who played Moana, would never have been tattooed if Flaherty had not staged the event (Calder-Marshall 113–14). Ta'avale endured the pain because he was well paid, and because, in Frances Flaherty's words, it "was not only his own pride that was at stake but the honour of all Samoa" (quoted in Calder-Marshall 114). This ritual of body tattooing is the subject of the seventh and final sequence in the film, yet Moana's tattooed back is evident when he is initially introduced, an anomaly that signifies the first of a chain of narrative inconsistencies that weaken the film's credibility. It actually took six weeks, not one evening as the film suggests, to cover his body from waist to knees with a patterned design, and from the expressions of pain on Ta'avale's face, we can assume that it was an ordeal for him. Next, a title attempts to give some credibility to what we see: "Through this pattern of the flesh, to you perhaps no more than cruel, useless ornament, the Samoan wins the dignity, the character and fibre which keep his race alive." However, this rite of manhood seems virtually meaningless within the community. Many of the other native adult men in this scene are not themselves tattooed, suggesting that there have been ways other than tattooing to keep the Samoan cultural tradition alive. Thus, the scene raises questions about Flaherty's approach.[48]

It is revealing of Flaherty's method to compare and contrast *Nanook*'s universal themes with *Moana*'s blandness. While we identify on a one-to-one basis with Nanook as a character, we cannot identify similarly with Moana. Nanook is an Eskimo father, as well as a father for mankind, and his concerns and instincts are those of all people. Moana is an adolescent, and while we empathize with his pain during the tattooing, there is virtually nothing universal in the experience. Flaherty's Samoan society, neither patriarchal nor matriarchal, seems to be one in which boys do the work of men. While Moana's father, a passive, older man, watches the tattooing, he plays no part in the tradition that it supposedly represents; except for dancing, the other men are little in evidence. Furthermore, while in *Nanook* conflict of man and nature is paramount, in Flaherty's Samoan world there seems to be no conflict of any kind; the benign behavior of Moana and his family diverts our interest from themes that are similar to *Nanook*'s, especially hunting, eating, and communal life.

Both *Nanook* and *Moana* were made in cooperation with their subjects, the Eskimos and the Samoans. But fictional as both films are in parts, *Nanook* more closely reflects Flaherty's greater involvement in and, consequently, greater understanding of Eskimo life. As Rotha (ed. Ruby) says, "For all its human feeling and warmth of approach, *Nanook* had a detached quality as if one were observing its characters from the outside. In *Moana*, Flaherty took the viewer in among the people to become one with them and no longer a detached observer" (76). In comparing these two films, it is evident that Flaherty's greater knowledge of the Inuit culture resulted in a more detached, objective record. *Nanook*, the more compelling film, reveals Flaherty's knowledge, while *Moana*, the more intimate one, reflects his fantasy.

Moana with one of Flaherty's daughters.

While the finished product of *Nanook* is Flaherty's alone, *Moana* reflects not only his, but also his wife's and his brother's ideas. Although Robert and Frances Flaherty continued to work together in various ways throughout his career, *Moana* is the only film they jointly signed; her name appears in the credits of other films, but never again as co-producer.[49] In 1959, thirty-four years after they left Samoa, Frances Flaherty appears to have

During the filming of *Moana,* Flaherty fell ill from drinking
water that had been poisoned by the chemicals used in
processing his motion picture film; too weak to walk, he was
carried to medical attention by natives.

acknowledged that the film is deeply flawed in preconception and realization, and to have dissociated herself from it. In the following somewhat
contradictory account, she ascribes the problems to Flaherty's approach,
offering some advice of her own about preconception:

> When finally he [Flaherty] had to admit that they simply were not there, I
> remember the miserable weeks and weeks he just sat on our veranda with
> every thought falling away from him, learning the first hard lesson of what it
> takes to make a *true* film of a subject you do not know: that you cannot
> preconceive. If you preconceive you are lost, off to a false start before you
> begin. What you have to do is to let go, let go every thought of your own,
> wipe your mind clean, fresh, innocent, newborn, sensitive as unexposed film
> to take up the impressions about you, and let what will come in. This is the
> pregnant void, the fertile state of no-mind. This is non-preconception, the
> beginning of discovery.[50]

In writing this statement, Frances Flaherty seems to have forgotten what
she wrote in 1925 about the integrity of their approach and their preconcep-

tions in making *Moana;* moreover, she seems to have forgotten the film itself.[51] Ironically, much of her 1959 account is essential advice for making a realist film and vital to direct cinema, the realist genre that comes closest to *re*-presenting reality. Even recognizing that beliefs and memories do not remain consistent, and that hindsight often brings insight, the discrepancy between what Mrs. Flaherty said in 1959 and what the Flahertys actually created from their Samoan experience is easily as wide as the discrepancy between what they found in Samoa and what they wanted to find.

IV

Moana remains important in Flaherty's canon because, as Grierson explains in "Flaherty as Innovator," it provided him with the time and opportunity for more technical achievement than was possible with the comparatively limited equipment he used in the Arctic (64–68). Brownlow wrote:

> The extraordinary richness of the photography of *Moana* . . . is due in part to Flaherty's use of panchromatic film. This has been portrayed as an accident, also as an innovation. In fact, it was neither. Panchromatic had been used by Hollywood cameramen for years. It was the staple diet of the old Kinemacolor process of Charles Urban. Flaherty planned *Moana* as a panchromatic picture from the beginning, probably under the influence of Charles Stearns Clancy, whose one independent production, *The Headless Horseman,* had been shot on panchromatic and was ready for release when Flaherty left. At the request of the owner of the Prizmacolor Company, Flaherty took a Prizmacolor camera; like all additive processses, Prizma depended upon panchromatic film. But the story that the color camera broke down and Flaherty loaded his Akeley with the panchromatic stock as an experiment is a denial of his wide knowledge of photography.[52]

Not only was Flaherty able to shoot with the color-sensitive panchromatic stock, but he was also able to use a larger variety of lenses than before. In "Filming Real People," Flaherty wrote:

> It was in the South Seas while I was making *Moana* that I first became aware of the peculiar virtues of the long focus lens. Of course, the chief function of the telephoto is obvious—one can photograph objects at a great distance. Without the telephoto lens, most wild-animal photography would be impossible. I had used the telephoto lens on my first picture, *Nanook of the North,* notably in the animal episodes, such as the walrus hunt. In the South Seas, however, it was in filming intimate scenes, and particularly in making portraits, that I learned the true value of long focus lenses. I began using them to take close-ups, in order to obviate self-consciousness on the part of my subjects. The Samoans, I found, acted much more naturally with the

camera thirty or forty feet away than when I was cranking right under their noses—and in this I am sure the Samoans are not different from other folk.

But the elimination of self-consciousness was not the only good thing that came from the experiment. The shots, when projected on the screen, showed a quality I had never been able to achieve with lenses of a wider angle. The figures had a roundness, a stereoscopic quality that gave to the picture a startling reality and beauty. Almost all of *Moana* was shot with lenses of six-inches focal length and upward. (97)

Flaherty's films are often cited for their cinematographic beauty—Bazin refers to their "photographic splendor"[53]—but Flaherty's enthusiasm for his new lenses did not always result in shots that record all of the action necessary to convey their full meaning (for example, the *siva* dance of Moana and Fa'angase). The most striking example occurs when Flaherty's camera follows Pe'a climbing the tree, but does not tilt upward until the boy climbs out of the frame, an unnecessary disruption of a rudimentary principle of visual continuity.[54] Flaherty was shooting from seventy-five feet below with a twelve-inch lens, and considering that he was using the gyro-head tripod, he could have anticipated the need for tilting. Overall, *Moana's* visual variety is rich in high-level shots, beautiful close-ups (especially Moana's mother making cloth), and extensive use of the moving camera.

Although the credits list Julian Johnson as the editor, Robert and Frances Flaherty edited *Moana* and wrote the intertitles; the editing and titling styles clearly resemble Flaherty's work on *Nanook* and show no evidence of new or different hands.[55] The intertitles of *Moana,* written in the slightly archaic and sometimes coy style of those in *Nanook* and *Man of Aran,* are used for explanation, dialogue, and comment, and can sometimes accomplish what the photography and editing do not. The Flahertys did not use editing in a traditional manner—for example, to cut from one shot to another to reveal something that the previous shot did not—nor, by the absence of editing, did they preserve realistic time and space. Examples of faulty editing include Moana's introduction with his back already tattooed, the many poorly matched shots, the confusing jump cuts to unidentified people, and the action within unedited scenes that does not justify their length. They did not edit their 240,000 feet of film until they had returned to Hollywood, and thus could not shoot additional footage they might need. Later, in *Man of Aran,* Flaherty edited some of his footage on location. Missing in Samoa was what Helen Van Dongen insisted on still later in the making of *Louisiana Story:* an attitude toward shooting that was oriented toward editing and a careful review of the rushes as soon as possible after shooting to determine if additional shooting would be necessary.

V

While Paramount executives—including Jesse Lasky, Adolph Zukor, and Walter Wanger—were enthusiastic about the first cut of *Moana,* they asked Flaherty to make it shorter. Although Flaherty complied, Rotha (ed. Ruby) observes that he then had a difficult time in persuading Paramount to release *Moana* (71–73). Paramount's attitude toward the film and its box office prospects was best expressed a little over a year later, in February 1926, when it released the film at New York's Rialto Theatre under its first title: *Moana: The Love Life of a South Sea Siren.* This original subtitle, since replaced with "A Romance of the Golden Age," ignores the film's narrative and shifts the emphasis away from Moana to his fiancée. In promoting the film for its romantic qualities, Paramount not only misunderstood the film, but also misjudged its audience potential for those seriously interested in other cultures.

If *Moana* falls short of fulfilling the promise established by *Nanook*—the fulfillment of which would have been another major achievement for Flaherty—it nonetheless pleased the critics (Murphy 62–66). It is most famous as the film to which John Grierson first applied the term "documentary"; in "Flaherty's Poetic *Moana*" (1926), he wrote: "*Moana,* being a visual account of events in the daily life of a Polynesian youth, has documentary value" (25). As we now realize, Grierson was not using the term as he later used it, to mean a film with a particular socio-political statement, but rather in the sense of the French word *documentaire,* used to describe travel or expedition films. Looking back in the 1970s, Grierson had second thoughts about the word "documentary" itself:

> I suppose I coined the word in the sense that I wasn't aware of its being used by anybody else. I mean, to talk about a documentary film was new, and I know I was surprised when I went over to Paris in 1927 and found them talking about "*films documentaires.*" Now, I must have seen that before, but I wasn't aware of it. When I first used the word "documentary" of Bob Flaherty's *Moana,* I was merely using it as an adjective. Then I got to using it as a noun: "the documentary"; "this is documentary." The word "documentary" became associated with my talking about this kind of film, and with me and a lot of people around me. There was a period (I think you'll find some very curiously mixed evidence on this subject) when some of them tried to get rid of the word "documentary," because it was felt to be very ugly. And Caroline Lejeune in *The Observer* kept saying, "Why the devil do we hang on

to this gruesome word 'documentary'?"; I said at the time, "Well I think we'd better hang on to this word because if it's so ugly nobody will steal it." And that, of course, is what happened. It was so ugly that nobody would steal it.[56]

In the years following its release, Grierson loyally praised Flaherty's achievements *(Grierson on Documentary* 139–44; 148–49), yet in citing *Moana's* "documentary value," he created an issue, as he later acknowledged, that he could hardly have anticipated. Closer to a travelogue than to any other genre of the nonfiction film, *Moana* lacks the insights into human strength and behavior that made *Nanook* such a remarkable film. Early critics made an effort to find a stylistic pattern that might link *Nanook* and *Moana,* but it seems clear that *Moana* represents a diversion from the pursuit of cinematic discovery begun with *Nanook.*

Moana enabled the Flaherty family to live and work together in a beautiful place. But, as Vincent Canby writes, "beauty is full of peril for the film maker. It can make reality seem exotic by putting it at a distance" (1). Although the Arctic must have seemed as "foreign" to Flaherty as Samoa, he captured its beauty and reality in *Nanook,* and made it seem universal, not exotic. While he captured the beauty of the South Seas in *Moana,* it seems only exotic, not universal. During the time Flaherty spent in the South Seas, he was able to refine his intimate approach (his "innocent eye"), as well as to experiment with artistic collaboration, an approach with which he was not then or afterwards comfortable, for it appears to have been an obstacle to the caution, independence, and integrity of his individual approach.[57] Samoa provided an idyllic period for the Flaherty family, and an idyllic theme for *Moana,* but afterwards, in each of his major films— *Man of Aran, The Land,* and *Louisiana Story*—Flaherty returned to man's struggle with nature, the existential theme with which he began his career.

CHAPTER FOUR

White Shadows in the South Seas (1929), *Tabu: A Story of the South Seas* (1931), and *Industrial Britain* (1933)

The Inevitable Clash of Collaborators

I

The six years between 1926, when Robert Flaherty released *Moana: A Romance of the Golden Age,* and 1932, when he began *Man of Aran,* were important to his self-affirmation as a film artist. During this period, Flaherty was involved with several projects that contributed to his increasing understanding of his art. In these efforts, Flaherty was motivated by two forces that are often considered mutually incompatible: the desire to make films independently and the desire to make money in the lucrative business of motion pictures. He wanted to make films his own way, to develop them from ideas that he would keep in his head throughout production rather than setting them down in an outline or a scenario. By giving cinematic expression to his spontaneous verbal gifts as a storyteller, he believed that he would succeed both artistically and financially.

In fact, although Flaherty had not yet learned that survival in the film industry is a matter of money first and art second, he did manage to survive, protected by his reputation, tenacity, and resilience. He enjoyed working, providing the Flaherty family's needs, and perhaps even acting out the image of the strong, protective father that is a constant motif in his films. However, he also spent his own and producers' money extravagantly, expecting others to pay his bills, a habit that was suited neither to the filmmaking industry nor to the independent filmmaker.

Flaherty's major projects during these years were *White Shadows in the South Seas, Tabu: A Story of the South Seas,* and *Industrial Britain.*[58] While the first two are of minor importance to his oeuvre, they involve Flaherty's collaboration with other directors and with Hollywood studios, and are thus relevant to a study of his methods of collaboration and to his work with John Grierson on *Industrial Britain.*[59] Two other films deserve brief mention: *The Potterymaker,* completed before *Moana,* and *Twenty-Four Dollar Island,* completed after. In 1925, under a commission from his friend, the actress Maude Adams, Flaherty produced *The Potterymaker* for the Metropolitan Museum of Art in New York City. Although this brief film shows Flaherty's appreciation of the artisan's craftsmanship, a concern that is evident in all his films and that prefigures a theme of *Industrial Britain,* it is little more than a rough sketch. In the same year, he made *Twenty-Four Dollar Island* (released in 1927), also privately sponsored, a film in the tradition of Paul Strand's and Charles Sheeler's *Manhatta* (1921). *Twenty-Four Dollar Island* is also a rudimentary study that attempts to capture the excitement of Manhattan's skyscrapers and harbor.[60] Within the context of Flaherty's work, it has significance as his first and only film wholly devoted to an urban subject, and he understood the potential in the subject even if he was not able to fully realize it. He said:

> I shot about thirty thousand feet, which will be boiled down to about two thousand, but really I don't know what I have got. But this I do know, it is a great idea for a picture and somebody is going to make a great picture of it one day. I'd like to have three years to devote to it. Yes, it would take that long to do it right. (quoted in Brownlow 484)

As Flaherty predicted, subsequent films have memorably captured the rhythms of Manhattan (among them, Willard Van Dyke's and Ralph Steiner's *The City,* 1939, and Francis Thompson's, *N.Y., N.Y.,* 1957); but Flaherty's fifteen-minute film was the first, providing New York audiences with a foretaste of two contemporary European "city symphony" films: Walther Ruttmann's *Berlin: The Symphony of a Great City* (1927) and Alberto Cavalcanti's *Rien que les heures* (1926).[61]

II

Despite the complexities of filmmaking—perhaps because of them (as well as the question of authorship)—collaboration between film directors is rare. The coupling of two names in the directorial credits usually implies one of two things: the producer either believed from the first that the

Flaherty, in 1927, at age 43, departing by train for Hollywood
to begin production of *White Shadows in the South Seas*.

talents of the principal director should be supplemented by those of a
second director, or he has fired the original director and replaced him with
another.[62] It was for the first of these reasons that producer Irving Thalberg
in 1927 asked Flaherty and John McCarthy to co-direct a film for M-G-M.
The story was to be based on Frederick O'Brien's *White Shadows in the
South Seas* (1919), the book that had helped inspire Flaherty's *Moana*.

Flaherty (standing second from right) and others in the *White Shadows in the South Seas* company being greeted by M-G-M officials on arrival in Tahiti.

Already an industry veteran at twenty-eight, Thalberg was accustomed to working with directors and producers who could accommodate their individual talents to the overall needs of their studio. Although Flaherty, at forty-three, had already had the unpleasant experience of making *Moana* for Paramount, he was not prepared for what M-G-M, Hollywood's most industrialized operation, demanded from a director. When McCarthy refused to co-direct with Flaherty, Thalberg replaced him with W. S. Van Dyke II, an M-G-M staff director known for his efficiency and versatility.[63] According to Brownlow's excellent account of the film's production, Frances Flaherty was not enthusiastic about this arrangement, but Flaherty stayed with the project and sailed for Tahiti in early summer 1927 (491–99).

Flaherty's contribution to *White Shadows* was miniscule—he had little to do with the script, less with the cinematography—but the film is relevant to an assessment of his work. It provides an example of his refusal to compromise about material that was important to him, and it shares motifs with both *Moana* and *Tabu*. *White Shadows* tells the story of Dr. Matthew Lloyd, a derelict who is ashamed of what the white people have done to the natives of a South Seas island. The white shadows of the title represent man's greed. The white men place the value of pearls above the value of human life, and they mock Dr. Lloyd for wasting his time in trying to save a diver whose lungs have burst. Watching a native girl shimmying for a drunken white man, Lloyd exclaims: "Civilization! God!" After being shanghaied and shipwrecked, he swims ashore and collapses, awakening to find a grotto of lovely women. Eventually the other natives welcome him into their lives, and he becomes a sort of god to them. The fast-paced narrative establishes motifs in the first half that recur in the second. For example, as Dr. Lloyd once massaged a diver to save his life, the natives now massage Dr. Lloyd to help him recover. He tries to revive a native who has apparently drowned, and this time succeeds in saving the man's life. When Dr. Lloyd himself, however, becomes greedy for pearls and prays that a ship will rescue him from this island, he is saved by the love of a native girl. But an old foe invades the island, establishes a trading post and bar, and kills Lloyd. As the film ends with a scene of drunkenness and debauchery, a native elder comments: "We welcomed them with our hearts. They have given us death."

Some activities in the film resemble those seen in *Moana:* the preparation of the feast in Lloyd's honor, the gathering of coconuts, the catching of the turtle, octopus, and fish. But Van Dyke did not seek to repeat *Moana's* romantic vision of the simple life. Through the theatrical exaggeration of its love story, *White Shadows* expresses a cynical vision of colonial activities and of the futility of preserving native cultures from outside influence. Life is hard, the sea is cruel, and the battle to maintain racial integrity is doomed to failure. The white characters of his film resemble similar characters in Somerset Maugham's short stories about the South Seas. These outcasts have the psychological validity that comes from a true observation of human nature, and their activities reflect the historical inevitability that Flaherty ignored in making *Moana.* The film is also more faithful to the struggle of man with nature. This is a paradise, but, unlike that depicted in *Moana,* a paradise with peril. The real dangers include the sharks, giant clams, and other hazards that divers risk for small wages to enable white traders to prosper.

From the beginning, *White Shadows in the South Seas* was the wrong project for Flaherty. He would not have chosen this material for himself, and it seems inevitable that he would soon become disillusioned and have little to do with the film's actual production. In Tahiti, his relations with Van Dyke and the rest of the crew rapidly deteriorated, and Flaherty returned to Hollywood in early 1928 (Langer 46). Despite this, the film eventually carried his name in the titles.[64]

III

At this juncture, there was little reason to believe that Flaherty and Hollywood would ever again sustain a working relationship, yet by June 1928, he had secured an agreement with the Fox Film Corporation to make a film about the Acoma Indians of New Mexico (Langer 46–49). As Flaherty had done with *Moana,* he planned to collaborate with his wife Frances and brother David. The temporary title of this drama of Indian life was "Nanook of the Desert," and Flaherty stressed that human life was even more precarious in the Southwest than in the Arctic. In their daily struggle for survival, the Acoma Indians faced threats from hungry wolves, a lack of water, and hostile Navajos. The shooting script "Acoma" reflects an uncharacteristic attention to structured narrative, in all likelihood the influence on Flaherty of his collaborator Randall H. Faye. After Flaherty had completed much shooting, Fox abandoned what it considered to be an untimely project. Flaherty disagreed with studio officials on both narrative and casting, and Fox, which was then adjusting its production to sound, was reluctant to invest more money in a silent film project. Although Flaherty left the film, the "Acoma" script remains relevant to his next collaborative projects. The major male characters of *White Shadows* and *Tabu* are similar, and the story, told through the eyes of a young Indian boy, foreshadows the narrative of *Elephant Boy* and *Louisiana Story.*

In 1929, F. W. Murnau asked Flaherty to collaborate on yet another South Seas islands film (Langer 48–54). Like Flaherty during these years, Murnau was involved in several film projects. An admirer of *Nanook,* Murnau planned to follow his first American films, *Sunrise* (1927) and *The Four Devils* (1928), with a film depicting Eskimo life before the white man arrived in the north. He eventually abandoned that project, which Allan Dwan later made as *Frozen Justice* (1929).[65] Both Flaherty and Murnau had had their problems with Hollywood, and the opportunity to work together on a film of mutual interest seemed an ideal alternative to working alone within the studio system.[66] Murnau and Flaherty combined their talents, not to rebel against the system, but rather, as Langer observes, "to produce their own films within the production system, although outside a major studio" (61). They formed Flaherty-Murnau Productions, Inc., a partnership in which Murnau held controlling interest but which stipulated that each would be paid an equal weekly wage and share an equal percentage of profits.

If, as Jean-André Fieschi observes, "all Murnau's films should be read primarily as voyages into the imaginary" (719), Murnau's motive for including Flaherty on this Tahitian voyage must have been his desire to develop a strategy for producing independent films within the Hollywood studio system. Murnau was a perfectionist who needed all the resources of a professional studio to achieve his cinematic style. Flaherty, an observer of real people in real settings, had little interest in the expressive possibilities of the cinematic art. Thus, despite their agreement, which seemed to guarantee equal participation in the creative process, Flaherty and Murnau differed sharply in their approaches to making *Tabu*.[67] At the beginning of this project, Flaherty wrote several times to his wife that he and Murnau worked together perfectly.[68] However, after months of production problems, it became evident that they could not work together as directors. Murnau emerged as the shrewder of the two, taking full advantage of his controlling interest in their partnership and leaving Flaherty as a junior partner in debt. As Murnau took financial control, Flaherty complained of his colleague's "terrible German will." Thus humiliated and forced to accept a much lower wage, Flaherty was reduced to working on *Tabu* as a cameraman and laboratory technician.[69] The credits for *Tabu*, released one week after Murnau's sudden death in 1931, give some evidence of the Murnau-Flaherty partnership: "Told by Robert J. Flaherty" and "Directed by F. W. Murnau."[70]

Much has been suggested, by André Bazin, Robin Wood, and others, about the cinematic elements that link the work of these two directors. Indeed, there are several elements in *Tabu* that fuse elements from the earlier films of both: the moving camera, the use of symbols, the fascination with death by water, and the celebration of the human body, nature, and romantic innocence. But the elements that divided them are more significant. Murnau's expressionism cannot be reconciled easily with Flaherty's realism, and his *mise-en-scène* is too strong even for this involved, melodramatic story of a young couple whose love violates a taboo and ultimately causes the young man's death. This narrative, introduced by an old chief's scroll and carried along by a white man's diary, is divided into two parts: Paradise and Paradise Lost. The second part, with Murnau's beautifully developed mood of decadence, is far better, with its constant visual patterning of black on white. *Tabu* is rich in symbolism: the shadows, which serve as omens of evil (more mysterious and real than those in *White Shadows*); the play of light and shadow that emphasizes the conflicts between ideas and cultures; the pearls in the grotto, guarded by killer sharks; and the pearl of great price, Reri's virginity. It took Murnau's genius, especially for lighting, to give visual expression to the Murnau-Flaherty story, and, in the final analysis, the lighting is all. Since Murnau and Flaherty made *Tabu* in the South Seas, far away from the technical capabilities for making a sound film, it was shot as a silent film, and the soundtrack, which contains no spoken dialogue, was prepared and synchronized in Hollywood. Hugo Reisenfeld's Hollynesian musical score is equally synthetic, combining sources as diverse and as improbable as Wagner and Dvorak.

In *Tabu,* Murnau realizes beautifully his tragic vision of a closed island world suddenly opened by the darker forces of evil: secret taboos, unknown dangers beneath the sea, and decadent people from across the seas. It is not a vision that can easily be reconciled with Flaherty's view of a world where there is no human evil and where man almost always triumphs over adverse forces. Andrew Sarris wrote: "Where Flaherty expressed man's adaptability to nature, Murnau pondered on man's place in the universe. Where Flaherty was concerned with the rhythm of living, Murnau was obsessed with the meaning of life" (43). Each had a moral vision to impose on Tahitian society: Murnau's was the more intellectual, darker, and European, while Flaherty's was the more instinctive, optimistic, and American. Yet it was economic reality, rather than their antithetical moral and aesthetic visions, that determined who would prevail. Langer notes that

> economic determinants, such as those caused by distribution and production logistics, seem to have played an interactive role with individual creativity in determining the form of the film. Flaherty's increasing marginalization during the production of *Tabu* was proportional to his decreasing control over finance and the tools of production. (60)

Tabu remains a critical juncture in the careers of both Robert Flaherty and F. W. Murnau. As Langer says,

> For Flaherty, it was to be the last effort to work on a film distributed by a major American company, and the end of an attempt to make films for commercial U.S. release that lasted, sporadically, for nine years. For Murnau, who died shortly before the film's 1931 release, *Tabu* was to mark the termination and possibly, as Lotte Eisner claimed, the culmination of his career. (43)

Although *Tabu* did well at the box office, critics were puzzled by the directorial collaboration and believed, because of its visual similarities to *Moana,* that Flaherty had made the greater contribution. Other critical discussion has focused on such issues as the origins of the script and the extent to which Murnau imposed his own moral vision on the story of Tahitian society. However, Langer believes that the nature and extent of Flaherty's contribution was more extensive than has been generally realized (60).

Tabu represents another of Flaherty's attempts to achieve success in spite of factors—temperamental, artistic, and financial—that would ultimately defeat him. All of Flaherty's most disappointing efforts, indeed his only failures, derive from his determination to make one kind of film while his collaborators wanted another. Experiences such as those with *White Shadows* and *Tabu* did not succeed in deterring Flaherty from future collaboration or commercial ventures, as *Elephant Boy* would demonstrate. When he left Tahiti in September 1929, he was apparently leaving the American film industry, saying that "going through Hollywood was like going through a sewer in a glass-bottom boat."[71] However, unpleasant experiences with three Hollywood studios did not diminish Flaherty's desire to make money and only strengthened his desire to make independent films his own way. He was not to realize the latter goal until—after another unhappy experience with *Industrial Britain*—he began *Man of Aran* in 1932.

IV

In December 1930 Robert Flaherty moved to Europe, where he would work for nine years before returning to the United States to make *The Land*. Flaherty spent the first six months in Germany, working on ideas for independent films and stimulated by the work of such European directors as Joris Ivens, Sergei Eisenstein, and Vsevolod Pudovkin. But Flaherty could not obtain German support for any of his film projects and so moved to England. There, largely due to Frances Flaherty's intercession on her husband's behalf, John Grierson offered him an opportunity to make a film.

The British documentary film movement originated in the work of the Film Unit of the Empire Marketing Board (E.M.B.), which between January 1930 and July 1933 grew from a minor to a major operation.[72] Before the government closed down the E.M.B. in 1933 and transferred its documentary filmmaking activities to the General Post Office, the E.M.B. Film Unit had produced over one hundred films. Grierson's concept of the social documentary prevailed in these films, which were distinguished as a collective effort rather than by the particular style or vision of one filmmaker. In *Grierson on Documentary,* he wrote:

The documentary idea, after all, demands no more than that the affairs of our time shall be brought to the screen in any fashion which strikes the imagination and makes observation a little richer than it was. At one level, the vision may be journalistic; at another, it may rise to poetry and drama. At another level again, its aesthetic quality may lie in the mere lucidity of its exposition. (22)

As the European and American approaches to the nonfiction film developed, it seemed increasingly likely that Robert Flaherty and John Grierson would one day work together, but it was also inevitable that they would clash. Although there was a great personal affinity between these two pioneers, they were very different, and neither altogether accepted the other's approach to filmmaking (Grierson, *Grierson on Documentary* 139–44). It was Grierson, the producer, who was to prevail. Grierson planned that Flaherty would act as a master teacher, inspiring the younger filmmakers in the fledgling British documentary movement with his gift for observation and his instinctive handling of the camera.[73] He also hoped that Flaherty's name would enhance the reputation of the group. As Brownlow suggests, the British filmmakers found Flaherty's films more important for their inspirational effect than for their integral artistic value (471).

Flaherty was attracted by Grierson's proposal to make a film about the relationship between individual British craftsmanship and Britain's industrial output, but, from the beginning of the project, there were temperamental and theoretical differences between the two men. While Grierson was not worried at first about Flaherty's disregard for such practical factors as finance, he was also not prepared for the problems this would bring. When Grierson remarked that an E.M.B. administrator would expect to see a script, Flaherty replied: "That's impossible. I've never written a script before and I'm damned if I'm going to start now for some civil servant in Whitehall."[74] Grierson said: "The differences were, of course, all rooted in our difference of economic approach. . . . He had an apparently innocent belief—I didn't think it was innocent—that there was always more money where that first lot came from" (quoted in Hardy, *John Grierson* 67).

In order to complete a coherent documentary film within the allotted budget, Grierson had no alternative but to dismiss Flaherty and finish the film himself.[75] Grierson had provided a budget of approximately $12,000 for production, more than was spent on any other E.M.B. film with the exception of the first, Grierson's own *Drifters* (1929). By contrast, *Night Mail* (1936), a far more ambitious film, perhaps the most successful aesthetically of all British documentaries, cost about $8,600.[76] Even with this substantial budget, Flaherty wasted funds.[77] Instead of traveling to several of England's industrial cities and settling down for a while in one or more of them, following his characteristic habit of slowly absorbing the culture and letting a story emerge, he shot film so rapidly that he used most of his entire allotment of stock on what he called "tests." Much of this footage was eventually used in *Industrial Britain,* but with additional photography shot, after Flaherty left the project, by Basil Wright, Arthur Elton, and even Grierson himself. In fact, Flaherty shot so much footage that Grierson was able to make five additional short films from the outtakes. Although this reclamation of footage was not part of the original plan, it served to justify both the budget and Grierson's faith in Flaherty.[78]

While *Industrial Britain* provides the sole opportunity to study the work of these two men on a single film, the final result reflects Grierson's contribution more than Flaherty's. The credits read, "Production/Grierson–Flaherty," but it was edited by Grierson (with the assistance of Edgar Anstey), who also added the soundtrack of commentary and music. The qualities of *Industrial Britain* that most clearly identify it as Flaherty's work are its beautiful photography and concern with craftsmanship. Flaherty's photography is characterized by his own trademarks of beautifully framed images and close-ups and very simple lighting, but it also reflects Murnau's influence in the moving camera and play of light and shadows on the men's faces and their machines. The theme of the film—"the old changes, giving place to the new"—underscores the shift in industrial production from the steam to the steel age. The film's structure—Part I, Steam, and Part II, Steel—is meant to embody this theme, but the transition of ideas is less effectively realized than the confident narratorial voice assumes. Linking these two periods in the industrial evolution of England is Flaherty's attention to the human factor, the craftsmanship and care that distinguish British products as diverse as coal, pottery, and glass. These products stand, in the narrator's words, "for the continuity of English craftsmanship and skill, for an emphasis on quality, which only the individual can give." Flaherty's images reveal a personality and dignity in the craftsmen that all the narrative about the "man at the lever" fails to communicate. However, even though the narrator asserts that "the human factor remains, even in this machine age, the final factor," Grierson's belief in industrial progress overshadows Flaherty's feeling for individual achievement. In this respect, *Industrial Britain* prefigures the subsequent *Night Mail;* both films attempt to relate the individual worker to the larger industrial process, to encourage workers' pride in their work, and to bolster their morale.

Industrial Britain was released in 1933 with a package of six other E.M.B. films, all of which were widely shown. Forsyth Hardy wrote: "Coupled with Grierson's ceaseless propagandising, in Whitehall, in the public prints and in lectures all over the country, they demonstrated that documentary was something more than a theory."[79] However, when *Industrial Britain* is contrasted with *Night Mail,* which is only two minutes longer, it is apparent how richly Grierson's concept of the documentary film was to grow in the five years that separate them. Although *Industrial Britain* is a simple film, its British fussiness nonetheless dominates, with pompous narration and insistent music providing a dramatic treatment that the subject neither needs nor warrants. Moreover, in his attempt to praise British industry and workers, Grierson overlooked several important factors. This is a film celebrating workers; but however much they are praised, they do not speak directly about their work. Grierson affirms man's freedom to work but seldom acknowledges his right to freedom of speech. As in many other British documentaries, *Night Mail* included, we learn about the workers only through the narration, and we never learn what emotions they might have other than what we are told about dedication and pride. The films that depict Grierson's Utopian vision of Great Britain share a reluctance to give voice to all who might have something valid to say about the central issues of concern. In addition, *Industrial Britain* was made in order to show that beautiful results can be achieved among the belching smokestacks and behind the ugly walls; but in making this point while sanctifying work, it disregarded air pollution, then as now a dangerous threat to the workers' health and to their community development. In fact, the air pollution that we see in almost every exterior shot of *Industrial Britain* later became the subject of Grierson's *The Smoke Menace* (1937), and subsequent British documentaries also recognized urban environmental problems.

Industrial Britain provides another example of what can happen when two different approaches to filmmaking are brought together with one eventually dominating over the other. Although the subordinated style comes through almost in counterpoint to the dominant one, the end result is confusion, not fusion. Grierson wrote in "Robert Flaherty" of their work together:

> When [Flaherty] made *Industrial Britain* with me, his flair for the old crafts and the old craftsmen was superb, and there will never be shooting of that kind to compare with it; but he simply could not bend to the conception of those other species of craftsmanship which go with modern industry and modern organization. (n.p.)

That, of course, was his theme in *Industrial Britain:* the old ways must change, giving way to the new, but the old ways are good ways, careful ways, and must be preserved, respected, and nurtured if there is to be a continuity of tradition. Flaherty was clearly interested in the individuality of British craftsmen and the worth of their work, but Grierson's way of filmmaking was not his. As always, he did not seem happy working within an organization, planning his films in advance, preparing to shoot with an eye to what the editor might need, or keeping the accounting records required by bureaucrats. Although Grierson was new to the business of filmmaking, he had shrewd judgment and tight control over the films produced under his name. When he saw that Flaherty could not fulfill his expectations, he had the courage to dismiss him. For the third time in five years, Flaherty had been sought as the master by a younger man, who then dismissed him, a humiliating series of disappointments that surely must have confirmed his desire to make films his own way.

Their differences did not deter Grierson from appreciating Flaherty's true importance as an artist and citing Flaherty, Méliès, Griffith, Sennett, and Eisenstein as the five great innovators in the history of film. In "Robert Flaherty," he wrote:

> Flaherty, great personal story teller as he was, did not especially think of the film as a way of telling a story, developing a drama, or creating an impact, either physical or mental. For him, the camera was veritably a wonder eye, to see with more remarkably than one ordinarily saw. (n.p.)

Subsequently, Grierson affirmed his admiration and their friendship by recommending the project that became *Man of Aran*.

V

From his experiences between 1926 and 1932, important transitional years, Flaherty realized both what he wanted to do and what he could do. First in Hollywood and then in London, he had found that the old ways did not work in the motion picture industry. He had a wonderful eye for observing life around him, yet he had little success when it came to choosing what projects would be suitable for him. Except for cinematography, he was impatient with the other technical aspects of filmmaking and continued to believe firmly in the unaccompanied visual image. He discovered that both success and money eluded him in collaborative work, and that in the future he had to go his own way. Perhaps, too, he discovered that his temperament was better suited to making films in the unspoiled spots still left in the world, where he could indulge his imagination, rather than in the cities, where inevitably he would have to face the unpleasant aspects of modern life that he so disliked. During these years, and through these experiences, Flaherty affirmed a vision of the world that was original, however ingenuous and wistful it might have seemed. He retained a steadfast belief in himself.

Between 1932 and his death in 1951, he made only four films. In two of them, *Elephant Boy* and *The Land,* working for producers with whom he disagreed, Flaherty repeated mistakes made earlier in *White Shadows* and *Tabu.* But in the other two—*Man of Aran* and *Louisiana Story*—Flaherty was faithful to his vision, again expressing his belief in a simpler, timeless state of existence, where, by the director's fiat, human hurt and suffering were absent.

CHAPTER FIVE

Man of Aran (1934)

Realism and Lyricism

I

If *Nanook of the North* and *Louisiana Story* are, respectively, Robert Flaherty's most personal and most fully realized cinematic achievements, then *Man of Aran* is his most powerful and poetic film about man and nature. *Nanook*'s success brought Flaherty great critical and personal reward, but he turned away from the purity and integrity of the *Nanook* approach to make films that were not only different from *Nanook,* but also less successful: *Moana: A Romance of the Golden Age* (1926), *White Shadows in the South Seas* (1929), and *Tabu: A Story of the South Seas* (1931). With *Industrial Britain,* a social documentary film in the Grierson tradition, he was drawn even further from his original approach.

It is, therefore, ironic that it was John Grierson who suggested that he make a film in the Aran Islands and that this was the film about man and nature that Flaherty had been trying to make for ten years. Although Grierson was committed to making British documentary films that would serve society, he knew firsthand that Flaherty was more interested in the timeless struggle of man against nature than he was in the short-range social situation presented in such films as *Industrial Britain.* As we have seen, Grierson wanted to praise the working class, to improve social conditions, and to use the dramatic possibilities of film to educate, while Flaherty wanted his films to ennoble mankind, to reveal tradition and culture, and to foster human understanding. Although fundamental philosophical conflicts continued to separate them, Flaherty and Grierson remained friends until Flaherty's death.

Beyond Grierson's original suggestion, Flaherty had other reasons for choosing the Aran Islands for his next film. Ireland was the country of his ancestors, and he was interested in its history and geography. The Aran

Islands and their inhabitants seem better understood by people with a poetic inclination than by those who are tourists or observers. Something of what Flaherty must have felt upon first seeing them is revealed in this description by William Troy:

> To anyone visiting the Aran Islands without a particular professional object in mind, their attraction is something complex and imponderable. It is not only the pinched beauty of their physical appearance—the precise network of minute green fields, the granite meadows the color of the sea, the hard-bitten contours of the coastline. It is not only the revelation of an economics so primitive that the very soil itself must be created by the hand of man—out of ground stone and seaweed laid along the barren slopes and ledges. Nor is it altogether the sense of a historical continuity such as one receives nowhere else in Europe—of a race which has been living in the same place and speaking the same language for more than two thousand years. All these impressions and feelings combine in the realization that here, on the fringe of modern industrial Europe, is a kind of little oasis in which both nature and man have managed to preserve an aristocratic indifference to the unruly passage of time.[80]

After several years of working on projects that fell short of his expectations, it was time for Flaherty to return to exploration and filmmaking on his own terms.[81] He found backing for *Man of Aran* in the British commercial film industry. The two major English film companies in the early 1930s were Gaumont-British Pictures, headed by Michael Balcon, and London Films, headed by Alexander Korda. At the time, British film critics were calling for more serious films, assailing the industry for relying too much on imitations of Hollywood fictional movies.[82] When Flaherty approached Balcon with the proposal to make the Aran Islands film, his primary reason appears to have been the desire for financial and critical success. However, Balcon accepted Flaherty's proposal in the belief that it would bring distinction and perhaps even profit to the company, a hope that Alexander Korda was to have several years later when he asked Flaherty to make *Elephant Boy*. Flaherty seems to have forgotten that he had dissociated himself from the commercial film industry after his conflicts with Hollywood over *White Shadows in the South Seas* and *Tabu: A Story of the South Seas*. Once again, he expected both to go his own way and, despite that independence, to profit. Considering his previous conflicts with the commercial film industry, his continued indifference to its economics is remarkable (Murphy 26).

Flaherty seemed determined from the start to find (or to invent) a story that would embody the conflict between man and the great sea that surrounded the Aran Islands. He sought to discover in these islands the epic theme that had preoccupied him since making *Nanook*—as Calder-Marshall wrote—"people who in the midst of life were always so close to death that they lived in the moment nobly" (67). He prepared for making *Man of Aran* by reading two works by John Millington Synge, both based on Synge's visit there in 1898: the one-act tragedy, *Riders to the Sea* (1904), and the nonfiction book, *The Aran Islands* (1907).[83] In the latter, Synge gave a direct account of his observations, "inventing nothing, and changing nothing that is essential."[84] While Synge's travel book may have provided the facts, *Riders to the Sea* seems to have provided the inspiration, and *Man of Aran* invites comparison with that haunting masterpiece. In both, the lives of the islanders are defined by the raging sea that isolates them and the barren rocks on which they live. The surrounding sea, a fact of life, becomes, through the imagery of Synge and Flaherty, a metaphor for their inevitable fate. Flaherty, like his characters, was in awe of the sea's power: "The sea must never be denied its victim, otherwise it will claim the rescuer, too, for its own. It must have its victim" (quoted in Murphy 23).

The beauty of Synge's poetry derives from the fusion of realism and drama in his verbal imagery. Through the native vigor of his speech, with its simplicity, dignity, and elemental rhythms, he captured the universal rhythms of life and death. His characters learn through the direct, immediate experience of suffering. Flaherty's cinematic imagery also blends lyricism and realism, revealing a truth that his structural narrative does not. Flaherty was a storyteller in the bardic tradition; for him, art was essentially social in function, derived from the life, traditions, and ideals of the community that he celebrates. The bardic tradition is also an oral tradition, and it is not surprising that Flaherty had an innate love of language and gained renown as an informal raconteur; his bardic aspirations may also account for his shortcomings in the more formal shaping of cinematic narrative. Through his careful, long, and steady observation, Flaherty invents the past, offering it as a record of the here-and-now. Although *Man of Aran* is not altogether faithful to Man *or* Aran, it is a powerful work of poetic realism.

After some preliminary exploring of the Irish mainland, Flaherty settled in January, 1932, on Aranmor (or Inishmore), the largest of the three Aran islands that lie about thirty miles off the coast of Galway.[85] *Man of Aran* depicts the life of an island "family" whose members Flaherty cast for the film from residents. This family, which includes father, mother, son, and an infant in a cradle, is extended to include three shark hunters and three boat men.[86] Flaherty's narrative places them in dramatic conflict with the raging sea,[87] the film's most important "character," recalling that man's struggle with creatures of the sea or rivers is a motif common to several Flaherty films. For example, Nanook struggles with a seal he has trapped underwater and uses a harpoon and line to capture a walrus and bring it to shore; *Moana* works in dangerous waters with nothing but spearfishing gear to protect him; and, both in and out of the water, the Louisiana boy engages in a slippery tug-of-war with an alligator. In those films, the struggle between man and nature is balanced in favor of man, who at least has a chance to win. In *Man of Aran,* however, the struggle is the sea against man, not man against the sea; the sea is the stronger combatant and most frequently the winner. Following is a brief synopsis of the film.

II

Like *Nanook* and *Moana, Man of Aran* opens with a prologue in title form:

> The Aran Islands lie off Western Ireland. All three are small wastes of rock, without trees, without soil. In winter storms they are almost smothered by the sea . . . which, because of the peculiar shelving of the coastline, piles up into one of the most gigantic seas in the world.
>
> In this desperate environment the Man of Aran, because his independence is the most precious privilege he can win from life, fights for his existence, bare as it may be.
>
> It is a fight from which he will have no respite until the end of his indomitable days or until he meets his master—the sea.

This statement of theme is a fundamental feature of the realist approach: define the world and then show it. However, the theme is not borne out by the initial visual narrative, which depicts a peaceful setting. Flaherty cuts from a scene of the boy Mikeleen hunting for crabs in a tidal pool to a scene in a rustic little cottage where his mother Maggie, surrounded by chicks and lambs, is rocking the infant's cradle. The music underscores these two peaceful scenes, but then abruptly Flaherty cuts to shots of the waves building into a raging sea and the men rowing in to shore through the boiling surf. Although the boat is badly damaged, the men safely reach shore. Maggie runs to help her husband Tiger-King save the nets; these nets are one of the tools by which the family sustains its existence. As the family walks home along the shore, Flaherty's long shots of the magnificent rolling waves remind us that nature here is the true leading character.[88] The drama and excitement of the *mise-en-scène* are apparently real because the footage is of real action; there could be no faking the storms or the danger of navigating a small boat through raging surf to the safety of shore. Yet Flaherty's condensation of time calls this realism into question, particularly in the abruptness with which he depicts the calm surface of the sea change

The *Man of Aran* cast and crew assembled for a group
portrait; seated in the front row are Maggie (far left) and
Mikeleen; in the second row, Tiger-King (second from right);
in the back row, Frances Flaherty (far left) and Robert
Flaherty (second from right).

into a tempest. With this first sequence, Flaherty clearly and economically,
if not convincingly, establishes realistic context, characters, and conflict.

The second sequence opens with an intertitle whose minimal information and archaic syntax are typical of other titles in the film: "The land upon
which Man of Aran depends for his subsistence—potatoes—has not even
soil!" Although another card tells us that "man" of Aran searches the rocky
crevasses for soil, we see Maggie doing it. While Flaherty may be using the
word "man" in a generic sense, there is a consistent and typical male
chauvinism here. Throughout his films, Flaherty tends to ignore women's
concerns and includes women only to preserve traditional family life. A case
in point is Maggie's frantic attempt to gather the nets; although we never
know why these nets seem almost as important to her as the boat or the
men, we can assume that she contributes to their worth by helping to weave
and repair them. At the end of the film, the father and boy are photographed in close-up profile, but the mother is seen only as part of the
group, not as an individual.

This second sequence includes scenes of farming and boat-repairing as well as Mikeleen fishing from a cliff. With excellent photography and editing, Flaherty also explains the people's crafts and the shark hunting, but farming is the more interesting activity, as well as the more relevant to Flaherty's overall theme of man struggling against nature. In actuality, since there was no natural soil, the Aranmor inhabitants had to grow their basic stock of potatoes in sandy soil dug by the handful out of crevasses and fortified with seaweed hoisted in baskets up the sheer face of the cliffs to the planting beds. For the film, as Harry Watt recalls, Flaherty insisted on reviving this back-breaking custom, even though the islanders had long since stopped carrying the seaweed up in baskets on their backs and instead used donkeys for the hauling (Sussex 31). We see Tiger-King create a meager garden by clearing the rocks from the land and splitting them with a sledge hammer and other rocks. Flaherty shoots this scene in a clear realist style, photographing Tiger-King in relation to the background (that is to say in real space) and to the action that he is carrying out (in real time).

Here, as elsewhere, however, this adherence to cinematic realism is compromised by the film's musical score. Each blow of Tiger-King's hammer is accompanied by insistent commentative music. Three times we see the hammer descend, and three times we hear the studio-recorded sound effects and musical approximations. Here, striving to create a mood of nobility, John Greenwood's score overwhelms the simple human activity it underscores.[89] In contrast, in the following boat-patching scene, the music lightens the routine activity without overwhelming it. Another effect of the musical score is revealed when Mikeleen spots the basking shark. The suspenseful music prepares us, and then the boy sees the shark; then the music stops, giving way to natural sounds (e.g., studio-dubbed seagulls) that are faithful to the actuality of the scene.

In what must be one of the most acrophobic shots in cinema history, Flaherty photographs Mikeleen fishing from the edge of a high cliff. Death from falling is just inches away, yet the boy winds and unwinds his line with calm and control. Although Mikeleen is an experienced observer of nature, his face registers fear when he first sees the huge but docile shark in the water far below him. Since it is unlikely that he is seeing a basking shark for the first time, his fear seems unreasonable, but Flaherty is less concerned with the logic of human behavior than he is with building his theme. The shark exemplifies the dangerous sea to most people, and Flaherty exploits his audience's fear of sharks and other killers of the sea. But in suggesting, at the same time, that the basking shark is harmless, he is not altogether fair. Although their pacific nature makes man's struggle with them more of a sport than a life and death conflict, once harpooned, these sharks are capable of diving and thus sinking their captor's boat. By withholding this information in the cause of suspense, and subsequently inventing narrative incident, Flaherty all but negates the positive achievements of his realist approach.

Meanwhile, the men have gone out to the sea in pursuit of the basking sharks. Because common sense rather than imagination prevails here, Flaherty does not invent a rite of initiation similar to those found in his other films, even though Mikeleen, like Toomai in *Elephant Boy,* believes that he can measure up to what would be expected of him. By having the men prevent Mikeleen from getting into the boat, Flaherty retains the film's emphasis on the men's struggle with the sea. Like Alexander in *Louisiana Story,* who carries a frog in his shirt, Mikeleen carries a little crab in his hat from one day to the next; both are apparently intended as talismans against the evil forces in water—Alexander's, a protection against the spirits he believes to lurk beneath the bayou's surface; Mikeleen's, a protection against what he believes to be dangerous in the sea.

The first shark hunt, photographed from the shore where Maggie and Mikeleen keep watch, appears contrived, as, indeed, it was. To extend the film's dramatic conflict, Flaherty revived a method of shark hunting that had not been used for almost one hundred years before he arrived on Aranmor. He persuaded the men to learn for the first time in their lives the arduous task of working the old boats and handling the harpoons. From the later footage, taken from a boat at sea, it does not appear to be particularly difficult to harpoon one of these lazy sharks, although the possibility of being capsized or towed to the open sea adds an element of danger to the otherwise calm activity. Whatever the motivation—Flaherty's conviction and energy, the salary, or the fact that these sharks were not man-eaters—the men performed their new tasks with enthusiasm and apparent bravery. In the past, to cite another anachronism, the islanders' cottages were lit by lamps fueled by oil rendered from sharks' livers; now they were lit by electricity. For the film, Tiger-King's and Maggie's cottage is lit by oil lamps, even though we see electrical wires linking it to the island's newer source of energy.

This rapidly edited but repetitive sequence of shark hunting (images of the boat, men, ropes, harpoon, waves, and shark) prolongs the film but does little to enhance the basic conflict. Furthermore, the sense of elapsed time is so ignored that we do not have a clear idea of the minutes passing or of the amount spent in each of the segments of the hunt. Meanwhile, Mikeleen, his mother, and other villagers tend the fire under the cauldron in which the shark's liver will be rendered into oil. The seven men in the boat and the activity of those other villagers on shore suggest a communal event, yet this presents a problem in narrative logic. If this is a communal event, why then, in a later scene, are only Maggie and Mikeleen there to watch the three men trying to return to shore in a storm? Maggie and her son suffer their anguish alone, making us wonder about the whereabouts of the families of the other two men in the boat.[90]

The final sequence begins at night with hints of a coming storm, followed by Maggie's usual morning activity of gathering seaweed against the backdrop of a huge sea. The dark, powerful poetry of the cinematography here affirms, better than anything else in the film, the sea's brutal power and the islanders' determined ruggedness. When the sequence fully establishes the magnitude of this storm, a shot reminds us that the men are still far out to sea in a boat that seems useless against the huge waves. As the men slowly make their way to shore, Flaherty builds the most unforgettable and dynamic sequence in this film. The music stops, and there is only the sound of the sea and wind and the voices of Maggie and Mikeleen, who try to guide them with shouts from the shore. At that moment, Flaherty moves from the romantic world of musical drama to the real world of human strife. The juxtaposition of pounding waves and feeble shouts emphasizes the unequal struggle in the boat and the helplessness on shore. The towering waves and raging surf seem to open momentarily to give us a glimpse of this special hell. Eventually the boat is sacrificed, and the men swim in through the surf to safety; even though Maggie's husband is safe, she rails against their eternal enemy in a mournful, unforgettable cry. Maggie's lament, interrupted by her thanks for the men's safe return, deepens the impact of this experience, reminding one of Maurya's last words in Synge's *Riders to the Sea:* "No man at all can be living for ever, and we must be satisfied." Indeed, in this final moment, Flaherty captures the tragic mood of Synge's play. The beauty of the moment helps one to forget the unexplained disappearance of the other two men from the scene. The following summary of shots shows the rhythm of the final rapid sequence: sea, father; sea, boy; sea, family; sea, family against sky; sea, family against sky; sea, family against sky; sea, family walking toward home. The editing of this final sequence completes the structural unity of the film, and the family is once again together against the overriding image of the sea.

III

The poetic realism of *Man of Aran* has a power and validity that help to overcome the film's shortcomings in narrative, soundtrack, and music. We can criticize Flaherty's reluctance to develop the grammar of his cinematography and rhythm of his editing, his inflexible attitudes toward camera angles and positioning, and his reliance on buildup and suspense for overall narrative effect. It makes little difference, though, to analyze his films in this way, for Flaherty seems to have been fully aware of what he was doing. He trusted his own eye and technique, developing a style relatively free of influences from Griffith, Murnau, Eisenstein, Vertov, and others who had already extended the variety and expressiveness of the language of cinema.

One of Flaherty's major assumptions (except, perhaps, in *The Land*) seems to have been that the audience would accept his vision of the world without questioning it. This is a problem, however, primarily because his films combined elements of fiction as well as fact. Flaherty's decision to stage the shark hunt and the potato planting typifies a basic aspect of his style. While he always used images out of real life, he never hesitated to stage an event, as long as it was probable, if this would enhance the narrative that he imposed upon what he found. However, by reviving disused customs and by ignoring all but the mythic elements of island life, Flaherty created an incomplete and perhaps invalid picture of that life. Dudley Andrew defends Flaherty's overall approach:

> All these fabrications were calculated attempts to make the images on the screen breathe the truth of a way of life that goes beyond immediate appearances. Flaherty believed that appearances must often be transformed from life to the screen (indeed, events must be altered) if the equation of a man's life in his environment is to retain its essential significance. (108)

Such large anachronisms as the revival of hunting and farming customs require that we accept them for their fictional validity within the narrative rather than for their revelation of something beyond immediate appearances.[91]

Both *Moana* and *Man of Aran* rely for dramatic conflict on the reenactment of past customs, yet Flaherty fails to explain the importance of either the tattooing or the shark hunt. Aware that a full explanation might call attention to the restaging, Flaherty avoided it, perhaps assuming that the visual interest of *Man of Aran* would sustain audience interest.[92] By concentrating his narrative on a physical action no longer relevant to island life, Flaherty again avoided depicting accurately the physical and especially the psychological realities of contemporary life. As most critics of the film quickly pointed out, Flaherty preferred imaginary conflicts to actual ones. Flaherty also ignored the effects of such worldwide events as the economic depression of the 1930s, suggesting to the audience that the Aran Islands were as isolated economically as they were geographically. Oblivious to political matters, he also avoided the very real conflict on the islands between Catholics and Protestants; other civil conflicts, such as those between citizens and the police; and the exploitation of Irish tenant farmers by absentee British and Irish landlords.

IV

With *Man of Aran,* Flaherty continued to experiment with cinematography, and, to a lesser extent, with editing and sound. To his customary use of the moving camera, he added a finer sense of framing, camera positioning, and camera movement. And in adhering to traditional, conservative film grammar in his use of conventional establishing shots, followed by medium close-ups and close-ups, he also revealed a greater awareness of how the cinematographer prepares the footage for the editor. Nevertheless, as we shall see below, these advances were still not entirely effective.

While working on *Industrial Britain,* Flaherty had been introduced to a wider range of equipment than he had known before. However, his most significant cinematographic achievement on *Man of Aran* came from his continued use of and experimentation with the long-focus lenses that had characterized his visual style since he had first used the telephoto lens in the making of *Nanook.* In Ireland, he used a spring-driven camera, writing in "Filming Real People" that it was "simpler in operation than any other camera I had ever seen, and not much heavier to carry around than a portable typewriter" (98). He was especially pleased with its steadiness in accommodating the variety of lenses that he used: wide-angle, two-, three-, four-, six-, nine-, and eleven-inch lenses, and an enormous seventeen-inch long-focus lens twice as long as the camera. He claimed that he owed almost everything to these lenses, and with them he captured some of the most extraordinary sea footage ever recorded on motion picture film.[93]

Another achievement made possible by this equipment was the greater intimacy in the shots of people, reflecting Flaherty's care not only in the choice of actors but also in the selection of lenses with which to film them. Frances Flaherty assisted in the casting, about which he said: "We select a group of the most attractive and appealing characters we can find, to represent a family, and through them tell our story. It is always a long and difficult process, this type finding, for it is surprising how few faces stand the test of the camera" (quoted in Murphy 24). In the choice of actors, as in other aspects of the film's invention, other factors took precedence over realism. For example, the man who played Tiger-King was not an Aran

Islander, but an itinerant whom Flaherty thought handsome. Thus, the characters were not given individual identity, but were chosen for their typical traits and function as abstracts, known only as Man, Woman, and Boy.[94]

Except for *Tabu* and *Industrial Britain,* both of which began as collaborative efforts, *Man of Aran* marks the first time that Flaherty worked throughout production with a professional editor. Although Flaherty and John Goldman managed to work together, with Flaherty reluctantly returning to shoot footage that Goldman required, Goldman complained that the director had sensitivity only for the shot itself and not for its place within the overall rhythm and structure of the film:[95] "His feeling was always for the camera. This wanting to do it all *in and through* the camera was one of the main causes of his great expenditure of film—so often he was trying to do what could *not* in fact be done" (quoted in Calder-Marshall 151). It was not always possible for Goldman to correct the flaws resulting from Flaherty's reliance on the camera, but his use of parallel editing heightens the suspense and mitigates some of the cinematographic faults that are obvious to the careful viewer.[96] The parallel editing also reflects Goldman's and Frances Flaherty's interest in montage, another departure from pure cinematic realism.[97] Another problem outside Goldman's control was Flaherty's insistence on printed intertitles, most of which appear sporadically, some without coherent relation to the narrative. For example, it is only after the first hunt that a title informs us that the sharks migrate each year to the Aran Islands; an earlier placement would have enhanced the drama of the hunt. In continuing to rely on such titles, several years after sound had made them virtually obsolete as a form of plausible narration, Flaherty showed both his faith in the written word and his reluctance to adapt to the swiftly developing technology of filmmaking.

The immediacy and intimacy of the photography that create a realistic context for our interest are undercut by a soundtrack of dialogue and music that was an afterthought, not an integral part of the production. In *Documentary Film,* Paul Rotha rightly observed that *Man of Aran* "avoided all the important issues raised by sound. . . ." (107). Flaherty not only had a poor ear for sound, but he also lacked an appropriate budget for making *Man of Aran* as a sound film. Its entire budget was less than the cost of *Nanook,* a silent film made more than ten years before (Calder-Marshall 142). Thus, after shooting *Man of Aran* on location as a silent film, he had to work in the London studio to post-record and dub-in the sound effects, dialogue, and music. While this use of post-synchronous sound was an economic necessity, it unfortunately challenges all the realist conventions without achieving anything that is aesthetically significant except perhaps the substitution of music for narration, a choice that (in itself, nothing new) can be poetic and very moving. Moreover, it calls attention to itself in ways that disturb the realist context that Flaherty was trying to maintain. For example, when the boat is breaking against the rocks, we hear what sounds like mere sticks being broken in front of the microphone. Although most of the dialogue is unintelligible, there is value in the sound mix, as Barnouw points out: "Almost lost in the roar of wind and wave, they [fragments of dialogue] were used with exceptional skill—almost as an additional sound effect" *(Documentary* 97).

John Greenwood's musical score often exceeds the meaning evident or implicit in the cinematography. It is more than commentative, striving for a lyricism of its own when accompanying shots of the relatively peaceful life that the islanders lead on shore, and marked by larger tensions when underscoring the dichotomy of sea and land, life and death. Although the shark hunt is the central conflict in the narrative, there seems to be no continuity in the pattern of its musical scoring during the hunt; sometimes there is music, sometimes there is not. In the final storm sequence, the music announces the storm; the animals in the cottage sense it intuitively (a familiar Flaherty motif); then the boy becomes aware of it; finally, his mother, framed against the sky and raging sea, carrying her load of sea-weed, knows that the safety of the men is threatened by this raging natural monster. In this sequence, Flaherty allows the sounds of wind and waves to register by themselves, thus preserving both the integrity and the meaning of the scene.

V

The mixed critical reaction to *Man of Aran* introduced an issue that was raised in connection with the films that were to follow and, ultimately, affected overall assessments of his oeuvre: Flaherty's fidelity to actuality (Murphy 70–74). Fundamentally, critics were divided on the nature and value of his work. Some critics were not familiar with Flaherty's achievements in *Nanook* or *Moana* and did not know what to expect from his approach. Those expecting a treatment of a timely subject suspected that his attempt to make a timeless myth was as false as his omission of the island's contemporary problems. Others, aware that Flaherty had worked with Grierson on *Industrial Britain,* may have expected *Man of Aran* to be a social documentary. Critics who wanted Flaherty to show the struggle of man against man failed to appreciate his depiction of the struggle of man

Man of Aran had its première on October 18, 1934, at the
Criterion Theatre, corner of Broadway and 44th Street in
New York's Times Square.

against nature, and, indeed, overlooked the film's beauty. Although Rotha
understood Flaherty's strengths and weaknesses as a filmmaker better than
most critics, in *Documentary Film* he, too, faulted *Man of Aran* for its
avoidance of social and economic reality:

> Give to Flaherty his credits; and they are many. Acknowledge our deep
> obligation to his pioneer spirit, his fierce battles to break down commercial
> stupidity and the bravery of his struggle against the despicable methods of
> exploitation from which he has suffered. But realise, at the same time, and
> within the sphere of documentary, that his understanding of actuality is a
> sentimental reaction towards the past, an escape into a world that has little
> contemporary significance, a placing of sentimentalism above the more
> urgent claims of materialism. (107)

Nevertheless, even if Flaherty did not make use of all the potentialities of
the documentary cinema, in this film he achieved something closer to his
own aesthetics by depicting the human struggle with richness of expression
and sensitivity.

Robert Flaherty's *Man of Aran* is the story of a people's struggle with the sea, the source of life and death in their island world. His characters are not of heroic stature, nor are they symbols of suffering, meant to illuminate man's condition. In serving mainly to exemplify Flaherty's view of the world, they suffer without purpose and are denied a full perception of their condition. They triumph over imminent death through luck as much as skill. There would have been enough tragic conflict for any film in the grim reality of their bodies framed against the relentless sea, searching for soil, squabbling among themselves and with their distant foes, refusing to leave their inhospitable habitat for the more temperate mainland. But because Flaherty invents their story and controls their action, his characters are detached from the life their prototypes actually lived. We cannot share their fears or their victories, knowing that the shark hunt has been invented and that this particular conflict with the sea is unnecessary. The prologue states that the sea may inevitably claim them, but while staging a symbolic death would have been within the boundaries of Flaherty's invention, they lose nothing here except a small boat and some nets.[98] Flaherty's faith in mankind, as exemplified in the struggle and victory of the Aran Islanders over the sea, made him deny the tragic rhythm not only implicit in the film's narrative, but also evident in the islanders' view of life. In so doing, however, Flaherty also denied the ultimate realities of life and death on which *Man of Aran* was based.

CHAPTER SIX

Elephant Boy (1937)

A Lesson Twice Learned

I

By the age of fifty, Robert Flaherty had traveled both the Northern and Southern Hemispheres; sailed the Arctic, Pacific, and Atlantic Oceans; and gone across Europe by train from London to Berlin.[99] Through the six film documents of poetic realism that resulted from these travels, Flaherty had slowly and patiently observed ways of life that were different from his own. With each film, he sought a new location and a new adventure. His favorite places were faraway and exotic, but he also enjoyed the world's great cities, where he regaled friends with stories that came from his experiences and, more often, from his imagination.[100] For his films, Flaherty loved to tell stories of human endurance, and he created heroes, some of them based on actual people, to exemplify the qualities he admired most.

In 1935, he continued this great adventure by sailing to India to make *Elephant Boy* for Alexander Korda, whose London Films dominated British motion picture production in the mid-1930s.[101] The Korda stamp, invariably stylish, was created by three Korda brothers working together: Alexander as producer and head of the company; Zoltan as director; and Vincent as designer.[102] Alexander Korda's success, which can be measured both in financial and artistic achievement, can be partially explained by the fact that he made pro-British empire films that reflected the political conservatism of the times. Karol Kulik observes:

> Korda was, after all, a confirmed Anglophile who saw the Empire builders as the embodiment of all the most noble traits in the English character and spirit. In his films about the Empire he wanted to sing the praises of, as the opening titles of *Sanders [of the River* (1935)] express it, those "handful of white men whose everyday work is an unsung saga of courage and efficiency," "the Civil Servants—keepers of the King's Peace." During a time of

mounting Fascism, Korda saw this patriotic expression, this exaltation of efficient law and order meted out not by fear and tyranny but by love and understanding, as perhaps necessary counterbalance.

Not to be overlooked, these stories about the Empire were great, action-packed adventure yarns, infinitely cinematic and especially suited—thanks to their reliance on stock characters and stock situations—to international distribution. They also exploited another untouched audience market, the Empire itself.[103]

Although London Films had prospered with such extravagant productions as *The Private Life of Henry VIII* (1933) and *The Scarlet Pimpernel* (1934), Korda sought greater artistic prestige, and, according to Rotha (ed. Ruby), anticipated making films with internationally famous directors and actors with whom he had not yet worked (163). When Korda had first met Flaherty in Hollywood in the late 1920s, he recognized him as one of the masters of the cinema. Flaherty represented the kind of talent that Korda sought, and they began to talk about a film project in early 1935 (Kulik 186–89; Korda 118–20). Pleased to be offered travel and work, the two things he enjoyed most, believing that Korda understood him, and typically caring little about contractual details, Flaherty signed a contract that gave the producer supervisory power over him. With his control assured, Korda was able subsequently to step in at a point of crisis in the film's production and to complete it for release. At the outset, however, each man seemed to be getting what he wanted.[104] Flaherty had the opportunity to take another trip and to make another adventure film, and Korda had the prospect of another great film about the Empire. That this producer and this director would go halfway around the world, in the middle of the Great Depression, to translate into film a Kipling story about elephants reveals just how much the project must have meant to them.[105]

As one might have anticipated, Flaherty and Korda disagreed throughout the planning and making of *Elephant Boy*. They were as temperamentally and artistically incompatible as Flaherty and W. S. Van Dyke on *White Shadows* (which Flaherty quit), Flaherty and Murnau on *Tabu* (which is more Murnau's than Flaherty's), and Flaherty and Grierson on *Industrial Britain* (from which Flaherty was dismissed). How completely they were at odds about this film is revealed in this account by Michael Korda, Vincent's son:

> Flaherty was willing enough to go to India, and prepared to be interested in elephants. He endured several story sessions, in which Alex explained to him why the film must have characters and a plot if it was going to succeed, rather than being a straight documentary. Then Flaherty sailed for India with his

wife, having left behind the script treatment, which he had no intention of following anyway. Alex had promised him a year's filming, and he vanished into the jungles of the Maharajah of Mysore in pursuit of the elephants. (119)

Soon after arriving in India in February 1935, Flaherty rejected the script, and with his wife Frances and brother David serving as assistants, he began random observation and shooting in hope of discovering a new story. His waste of film soon alarmed Alexander Korda, and within the next eighteen months, many additional people became involved in the production. First, Korda assigned Monta Bell, a Hollywood director, to assist Flaherty. When Bell could not accomplish much, Korda sent his brother Zoltan to supervise. Eventually, three different English units in India had photographed independently from three different scripts. When Flaherty returned to complete the shooting in England in June 1936, he finally realized that the film was no longer his to control or complete.[106] In making *Elephant Boy,* Flaherty had once again encumbered himself with collaborators and prevented himself from finding what he had set out to explore.[107]

II

Independent of one another, and for some time before their collaboration on *Elephant Boy,* both Flaherty and Korda had considered making a film about boys and elephants. Frances Flaherty offers one account of how Flaherty came to make the film:

> Wherever we took our camera, from one primitive scene to another, we used the native people as our characters and took our material from the stuff of their lives. We found what good actors native children can be, and how appealing they unfailingly are to an audience. So we had this idea;—why, if we wrote a film-story around extraordinary adventures that a native boy might have in his native environment, wouldn't it be possible to "star" that boy himself in the film?[108]

This was not the first time that they had had such an idea. In 1929, the Flahertys wrote a short story called "Bonito the Bull," which recounted the actual adventures of a boy and his bull. Later, thinking that this story might be adapted for a film, they had the boy attach his affections to an elephant.[109] Coincidentally, Alexander Korda had been planning to make a film based on Rudyard Kipling's *Jungle Book* story of "Toomai of the Elephants," and he suggested that the Flahertys adapt the famous story.[110]

The stories in Kipling's *Jungle Books* (1894–95) represent a departure from the traditional kind of beast fable that attributes human qualities to animals; instead, they attempt to probe the psychological nature of animals. These stories, which are delightfully told, appeal to adults as well as to the children for whom they were written, with some of their charm deriving from the convention that grants speech to animals. Following is a brief synopsis of Kipling's story.

"Toomai of the Elephants" tells the story of Little Toomai, a ten-year-old boy, and Kala Nag, a legendary seventy-year-old elephant whose name means Black Snake. Like Kipling's other animals, Kala Nag has a strong personality. A splendid fighter, he is wise, has traveled across India and even abroad in the service of his country, and has been recommended for a war medal. He is afraid of absolutely nothing except his *mahout* (master), Big Toomai, father of Little Toomai. Kala Nag was determined never to be afraid because his mother taught him that elephants who are afraid always get hurt. Through his behavior, he imparts this lesson to Little Toomai, whose bravery and self-confidence protect him from harm at the turning point of the story.

Little Toomai works daily with his father, learning the tasks that he will eventually inherit along with Kala Nag, who has been in the family for three generations. The elephant operations of the British government are supervised by Petersen Sahib, whom Little Toomai regards as "the greatest white man in the world" (sahib is the title once used by natives in India when speaking to, or of, a European). When Petersen learns that Little Toomai has entered the *keddah* (stockade) and assisted the *mahouts* in a way that is more foolhardy than brave, he tells the boy that he can enter the *keddah* again when he has seen the elephants dance, a diplomatic way of telling him that he is simply too young for the dangerous work. Nonetheless, Petersen rewards Little Toomai with money, recognizing that the boy, in entering the *keddah,* shows great potential for his future as an elephant hunter or master. This makes the boy feel "as a private soldier would feel if he had been called out of the ranks and praised by his commander-in-chief." However, the hunters laugh at the boy, believing that he will never find the spot where the elephants dance:

> There are great cleared flat places hidden away in the forests that are called elephants' ballrooms, but even these are only found by accident, and no man has ever seen the elephants dance. When a driver boasts of his skill and bravery the other drivers say, "And when didst *thou* see the elephants dance?" (2: 157)

That same moonlit night, after the masters and elephants have settled down to sleep, Kala Nag breaks his tether and, with Little Toomai on his

Elephant Boy: Petersen Sahib (Walter Hudd) and Toomai
(Sabu).

back, heads up from the plains, through the forest, across a river, and finally
to a clearing, the elephants' ballroom. Here, hundreds of elephants, many
of them with broken chains still attached to their feet, are performing the
elephants' dance, stamping their feet and making trumpet-like calls through
their trunks. At dawn, Kala Nag and some of the other elephants, including
Petersen's own animal, return to the camp, where Little Toomai tells
Petersen what he has seen. Petersen finds the site and confirms the boy's
discovery; although it is the second time in his eighteen-year career that
Petersen has found such a place, he has never seen the dance. Little Toomai,
the only person *ever* to have seen this phenomenon, is celebrated at a feast,
where Petersen's Indian aide speaks:

> This little one shall no more be called Little Toomai, but Toomai of the
> Elephants, as his great-grandfather was called before him. What never man
> has seen he has seen through the long night, and the favour of the elephant-
> folk and of the Gods of the Jungles is with him. He shall become a great
> tracker; he shall become greater than I, even I—Machua Appa! He shall
> follow the new trail, and the stale trail, and the mixed trail, with a clear eye!
> He shall take no harm in the Keddah when he runs under their bellies to rope

the wild tuskers; and if he slips before the feet of the charging bull-elephant, that bull-elephant shall know who he is and shall not crush him. . . . Give him honour, my lords! *Salaam karo,* my children. Make your salute to Toomai of the Elephants. (2: 171)

Thus, Toomai, celebrated for seeing what no man has ever seen before, is recognized as a leader.

This Kipling story provided little more than the inspiration for John Collier's script for *Elephant Boy*. Collier, assisted by Akos Tolnay and Marcia da Silva, broadly adapted this little fable about bravery, placing more emphasis on the boy, less on the elephant, adding considerable action, and extending the time from one day to many weeks. Kipling's fantastic story, with its dreamlike rite of passage, is transformed into an action-adventure story in which Toomai has great powers. Set in the Indian jungle, in the context of tension between the Indians and their British rulers, the film tells the story of the boy's oneness with nature, his triumph over skeptical natives, and his recognition as an elephant hunter.[111] Following is a brief synopsis of the script for *Elephant Boy* with indications of where it varies from the Kipling source.

III

Elephant Boy opens with the turning pages of a leather-covered volume, a trite conceit that provides the major credits and reminds the audience that they are about to see the cinematic adaptation of a literary classic. Speaking as if to an audience of sahibs, Sabu introduces himself and explains the importance of the elephant to Indian life. Sabu's coy child-star charm may once have been appealing, if only for his exotic appearance and determined pronunciation of English, but his submissive manner, which includes a final bow to the audience, sets the tone and establishes the ethnic stereotypes that will prevail throughout the film.[112] After this awkward prologue, the narrative begins in a manner that is typical of Flaherty in its lyric establishment of place, character, and motifs.

Toomai, sleeping in the tall jungle grass, is awakened by his father's elephant, Kala Nag, who mimics his waking motions. This stretching, scratching, and eating—further mimicked in the behavior of a nearby monkey—suggests a oneness and equality, a co-existence of man and beast, both great and small. Toomai, in charge of the great beast, rides him to the river, where other elephant keepers tease him.

Elephants were then important in the daily life of India, but there is a scarcity of them in the region, and a shot of a poster informs us that the Mysore government is planning an elephant hunt to be supervised by the Englishmen in charge of such matters. Playing with the stiff-upper-lip reserve that is now seen as a caricature of white colonial behavior, these men recruit natives as hunters and bearers and hire Toomai's father and Kala Nag, an animal that has served the family for three generations. Little Toomai, who impresses the Englishmen with his skill in handling Kala Nag, is permitted to join the hunt even though he is officially too young to participate. Here the film makes two major changes from its source. Kipling rewards Little Toomai's bravery in the *keddah* with money, but the film permits him to join the hunt. Where Kipling depicts friendly relations between the British and the Indians, the British in the film condescend to the Indians, who nevertheless are evidently eager to have work.

The hunt gets underway, but after six weeks no elephants are captured, and the natives, who were once happy, smiling, and singing as they built the stockade, are now despondent and superstitious (all major changes from Kipling). Petersen is bewildered at the situation, but Little Toomai "knows" that there are elephants because he has listened to the "jungle men" (spirits with whom he alone is in touch). Natives and Englishmen alike mock him and his youthful pretensions to being a hunter, telling him that he can only become a hunter after he witnesses the elephants' dance. While the older men admit that this is "just an old tale for children," Toomai believes it.

In a tragic accident, Little Toomai's father is killed by a tiger (there is no such beast in Kipling's story). Toomai learns of the death by Kala Nag's braying (the elephant "understands" English as well as physical commands, foreshadowing Lassie's extraordinary powers of divination), and after burning his father's corpse on a funeral pyre, the boy seems to be unofficially adopted by Petersen. Since his mother is also dead (another change from Kipling), Toomai is now a boy alone in a man's world. Kala Nag, crazed with grief for his dead master and badly beaten by his new master, a native, goes on a rampage that destroys much of the hunters' camp. All of this was meant to illustrate the boy's coming-of-age as well as to add much action and excitement to the film. Only Toomai can tame the creature, but when he does, the hunters demand that the animal be shot to avenge the injury and damage that he has caused. But Petersen intervenes, saving the elephant and permitting Little Toomai to remain for the hunt rather than making him return to the village and school. This benevolent action, in contrast to the native master's cruel treatment of Kala Nag, is meant to establish the white man as a conciliator who brings law, order, and justice to the violent jungle. This impression, of course, is what the Kordas intended their Empire films to convey.

Toomai becomes Kala Nag's master, and together one night they slip away from the camp. Discovering a herd of wild elephants, they see the legendary elephant dance.[113] Eventually Petersen and the others locate Toomai and the herd, and organize a stampede and roundup of the beasts. The elephants of Toomai's moonlit discovery in the Kipling story are here a wild herd regarded as cattle for roundup. The charm and dreamlike quality of Toomai's initiation is transformed into an objective reality that benefits the local economy. The story ends happily as the hunters agree that the gods of the jungle chose Toomai to be an elephant hunter. After all, he found the secret hiding place of the herd and saw their dance, thus bringing them all prosperity. They salute him as "Toomai of the Elephants," at which he cries for joy.

IV

Elephant Boy shares motifs that are central to Flaherty's other films: the flow of life and the transcendence of human nature over human and natural obstacles; the love of nature and animals; the close relationship between fathers and sons (the variant here is that his father's death allows Toomai to go forward with what he has learned); the rite of initiation, which signifies manhood and brings the respect of society; and the necessity for man's belief in the "other," something beyond perception. White experience clashes with black intuition, and realism with idealism, variations on a theme that would have its fullest and most convincing expression in *Louisiana Story*. Flaherty typically avoids direct social comment or criticism. However, *Elephant Boy* is unlike his other films in that Flaherty yearns less for the past and, in his characterization of both the cruel natives and the imperious British, depicts human nature more realistically.

One fault of *Elephant Boy* is that its narrative perpetuates the myth of a strong British rule. By the mid–1930s, the rulers of the British Empire knew well the danger of ignoring the economic and social realities of their dominions. Flaherty, however, once again takes liberties with the culture that he is recording. Although he must have been aware that Indian nationalists were progressing toward independence from British rule, Flaherty preferred to create a vision of an earlier day, complete with stereotypes of confident and superior white men and their cheerful dark-skinned servants. Flaherty's presentation extends the imperialistic attitude expressed in some of Alexander Korda's earlier films. Indeed, the film contains elements of both Korda's and Flaherty's visions. Korda's tribute to British rule is expressed in man's capturing and taming the elephants; Flaherty's tribute to the Indians, and to man's natural independence, is manifest when these huge, wonderful elephants elude their British hunters for six weeks.

Yet another interpretation of the symbolism of the hunt is expressed by Petersen Sahib, who, in an astonishingly simple assessment of the situation, suggests that a "curse" is hindering the progress of the hunt. He can hardly be alluding to the actual anti-British sentiment, for the script is neither that subtle nor that ambiguous. Rather, for a jingoist like Petersen, British life in India is all success or failure, the British in the winning spot or cursed. Sabu's respect for the "other" amuses Petersen; in this attitude, Petersen resembles the men on the oil-drilling barge in *Louisiana Story*. Throughout, Petersen's character functions as a symbol of what, in actuality, was the fast-eroding presence of the Raj.[114] When the drama of action becomes a drama of revenge—at the point where Petersen intervenes and saves Kala Nag from being shot, an action in which the white man's mercy takes precedence over the black man's justice—Petersen shows a firm, albeit cruel, understanding of human nature. Once Petersen has made his decision, he prevails, and we do not hear again from the natives who have clamored for their own kind of justice. On the other hand, Petersen's character can become almost implausible, as when he has to be told step-by-step by the natives all about elephant behavior, a subject on which he is supposed to be the British government's expert. On the whole, his role in the film serves to reaffirm the power of the British Raj and contributes to the film's narrative, but it contradicts the reality of India at the time the film was made. Ironically, while British film critics criticized Flaherty for ignoring political and social reality in *Man of Aran*, they said almost nothing about his treatment of India, the impending loss of which was foretold by the 1937 election victories of the Indian National Congress. In the threatening world political chaos, perhaps their pro-Empire feelings took precedence over their social consciousness.

Another fault of the film is that it fails to respect the Kipling story from which it was derived. Flaherty sought a story that would emerge from India and the Indians as he observed them. Ironically, Kipling's slight narrative told a good story and should have afforded Flaherty abundant opportunities for creating his own magical world. Kipling's reader must use imagination to form a picture of the jungle and Toomai's night ride to the elephant dance. Knowing that Flaherty was associated with documentary realism, the film viewer accepts the images on the screen, and some viewers may find *Elephant Boy* believable because it does not look neatly constructed. However, in view of Kipling's achievement, the film's handling of narrative is disappointing. Still, Flaherty did not have final control, and it is not altogether his fault that the film's narrative lacks some of the qualities that make Kipling's story a classic. Where Flaherty insisted on mood, the Kordas demanded a story and made major script changes in completing the film.

Elephant Boy contains some lovely Flaherty sequences, but like his contributions to *Tabu* and *Industrial Britain,* these were not sufficient to give the whole film the familiar Flaherty style. His touch is evident in his affection for nature, in his treatment of the mutual love of the boy and the elephant, and in his affectionate direction of Sabu. The sequences shot on location in Mysore reflect Flaherty's careful, lyric observation of things: Toomai and the elephant awakening, Toomai's prayer to the colossal Jain statue, the construction of the stockade, and the exciting elephant stampede. However, to complete *Elephant Boy,* it was inevitable that Alexander Korda would substitute proven studio procedures for the personal approach with which Flaherty had produced *Nanook of the North* and *Man of Aran.* Expediency replaced authenticity, as white actors were unconvincingly made-up as Hindus; Walter Hudd was cast as Petersen Sahib, replacing Flaherty's friend Captain Fremlin; tame elephants were borrowed from a zoo; Sabu's English was improved; and studio sets replaced the real jungle settings with the neat, artificial ambiance of the back lot.[115] Osmond Borradaile's beautiful cinematography captures the light and shadow of the jungle, the imposing contrast between the boy and beast, and the camp in moonlight, but the lighting does not match in many of the jungle scenes that comprise a sequence, perhaps because it combines footage shot both in the actual jungle and in the studio simulation.

Although *Elephant Boy* was produced almost ten years after the introduction of sound, Flaherty originally conceived it as a silent film that would use narrative intertitle cards. However, Korda planned it as a sound film, and Flaherty shot fifty-five hours of film with the collaboration of the Korda sound technicians in India, including some synchronized sound and dialogue scenes. In London, Zoltan Korda shot additional material and reshot other scenes, paying particular attention to sound. Nonetheless, the film does not possess the convincing realism that sound recording could already achieve at the time.[116] In almost every way a hybrid creation, *Elephant Boy* reflects neither the innocent simplicity of Flaherty's earlier films nor the comparative cinematic perfection of the studio-produced films of the day.

Flaherty (standing left) directing a scene in *Elephant Boy*.

V

Elephant Boy is the result of a compromise between the different approaches
to filmmaking of Robert Flaherty, Alexander Korda, and Zoltan Korda.
While none of them could have made quite the same film alone, together
they produced an almost classic example of what happens when collaboration goes wrong. *Elephant Boy* lacks the stamp of an individual artist.
Identifying a discernible style is complicated further by credits that, in
addition to the major contributors, list William Hornbeck as "supervising
director" and David Flaherty as "assistant director." Certainly, the documentary value of the film reflects Flaherty's style, the glossy studio appearance reflects Alexander Korda's eye on the box office, and the entertainment value of the film reflects Zoltan Korda's interest. It is not known what
Hornbeck or David Flaherty contributed. And, in fact, Flaherty could not
have made *Elephant Boy* alone, for he would have been hindered by the
script, the sound recording, and the technical obstacles presented by jungle

and studio shooting. Alone, Zoltan Korda could not have given it the lovely Flaherty touches. Together, however, with Alexander Korda's support and his studio's resources, the film was completed.

Although *Elephant Boy,* signed by Flaherty and Zoltan Korda, won the award for Best Direction at the 1937 Venice Film Festival, it represents the lowest point in Flaherty's career as a film director.[117] The critical reception was mixed, with praise and blame divided between Flaherty and the Kordas.[118] Korda was successful and could easily survive such notices for one film, but Flaherty was far more vulnerable. *Elephant Boy* damaged his reputation and did little or nothing to advance him professionally. As a result of this and the experiences that he had already had on *Tabu* and *Industrial Britain,* Flaherty seems finally to have realized that the motion picture studios and their fiction scripts were not for him. He knew that in the future he would either have to follow his independent course or find collaborators who were more sympathetic to his approach. However, there were positive aspects for Flaherty in this Indian adventure: he had been fascinated by the beauty of India, he had been treated royally by the Indians and British alike, and he had enjoyed working with Sabu.[119] Nonetheless, his future looked bleak, and, suffering again what Rotha (ed. Ruby) called "the demoralizing frustration of unemployment" (184), Flaherty was in a dilemma over what appeared to be scant sources of funding for future projects. Both Robert and Frances Flaherty were worried about the threat of another world war, and, in September 1938, Mrs. Flaherty returned to the United States with their two youngest daughters. In the following months, with war imminent, Flaherty realized that all prospects of British or European film work for him had disappeared, and in July 1939, he, too, returned to rediscover his native land.

CHAPTER SEVEN

The Land (1942)

Arbitrariness Is the Enemy

I

In 1939, at the invitation of Pare Lorentz, Robert Flaherty returned to the United States to make *The Land,* his most personally revealing and most controversial film. Besides providing Flaherty with the opportunity to make a film about American agriculture, the project offered him, for the first time in his adult life, the opportunity to explore and discover the United States for himself. In many ways, this would appear to have been the wrong project, under the wrong circumstances, at the wrong time. Although the film was based on contemporary events, the American social situation was so changeable that the introspective Flaherty had difficulty in keeping abreast of it. The fragmentary nature of what was occurring in his native land is therefore reflected in the puzzle that is *The Land;* at the same time, Flaherty's uncertainty provides the film's essential honesty. In no other work did Flaherty seem so restless or question his values so deeply. Indeed, Flaherty struggled both with the bureaucracy and with himself in making *The Land,*[120] but the product of this struggle must have been of considerable value to him, for he said that *The Land* was his deepest and truest film (Strauss 199).

The Land was Flaherty's second attempt, after *Industrial Britain* (1933), to make a government-sponsored documentary film in the Griersonian manner. Government-sponsored filmmaking in the United States was short-lived even though New Deal support for such efforts as the Federal Arts Project, the Theater Project, and the Writers' Project were appropriate precedents for establishing comparable projects in film. In 1938, President Franklin D. Roosevelt created the United States Film Service (USFS), appointing Pare Lorentz to head it, but Congress—never comfortable with government-sponsored art, and particularly wary about films that criticized the existing social and economic order that they had been elected to pre-serve—discontinued its funding in 1940. At the time, Lorentz wrote: "if there ever was a [documentary film] movement, a school, a development, it is practically stopped dead in its tracks" (190).

While an organized, government-sponsored American documentary film movement existed only briefly, and primarily through independent efforts, during this short period Lorentz successfully introduced the Grierson approach through his three films—*The Plow that Broke the Plains* (1936), *The River* (1937), and *The Fight for Life* (1940); and through two films that he produced for the United States Film Service—Joris Ivens's *Power and the Land* (1940) and Flaherty's *The Land*, both edited by Helen Van Dongen. In the years immediately prior to the entrance of the United States into the Second World War, other American documentaries were produced, such as Willard Van Dyke's and Ralph Steiner's *The City* (1939); but these were not government-sponsored, and none of them—with the exception of those made by leftist groups—was the product of an organized movement such as existed in England.[121]

The Land was begun by the USFS for the Agricultural Adjustment Administration (AAA) of the Department of Agriculture. When Congress discontinued USFS funding in 1940, the AAA completed and released it, first for commercial theatrical release and later for screening at farmers' meetings. Lorentz originally intended *The Land* to be about the problems of rural Americans displaced by the interrelated phenomena of drought, poor farming methods, and poor management of farm production. He wanted to produce films that would show viewers what the Roosevelt administration was doing about contemporary problems. Lorentz pro-posed a bold treatment of the social problems that he had dealt with in *The Plow that Broke the Plains* and that John Ford represented eloquently in his film adaptation (1940) of John Steinbeck's *The Grapes of Wrath* (1939).

It is, at first, surprising that Lorentz would have invited Flaherty to make a straightforward propaganda film like *The Land* and that Flaherty would have accepted. The Flahertys had been living in England, but, in view of the threat of war in Europe, Frances Flaherty had already returned to the United States and was convinced that her husband should also return. She sought Grierson's help, and he, in turn, suggested to Lorentz that he invite Flaherty to make a film about American agriculture.[122] Flaherty was an independent filmmaker, temperamentally unprepared to participate in a group filmmaking effort such as the USFS, but, characteristically, he did not ask Lorentz many questions about the project, for return to America meant work for him and a reunion with his family. Although Flaherty was born in Michigan, he had spent most of his youth and early working years in Canada, and since 1926, had traveled extensively, making films throughout the world. Returning, he was faced with two challenges: reconciling his personal approach with the prevailing practices of the American nonfiction film, and reacquainting himself with a society about which he now knew very little and, especially, with what he called the "fierce, electrical violence of the American climate" (quoted by Russell Lord in Rotha, ed. Ruby 190). Although Lord observed that Flaherty was "baffled at the outset" (quoted in Rotha, ed. Ruby 191) by the country and the project, he had, as a boy, experienced pioneer life firsthand; he had seen natural and man-made disasters, and had known of families, their dreams shattered, forced off their land. From his experiences in depicting man's struggle with nature in such films as *Nanook, Moana,* and *Man of Aran,* Flaherty thought that he would not have any trouble making *The Land.*[123]

Flaherty's first objective was to explore the country and, in his customary manner, discover the story of the new film through observation. He, his wife, and his crew made three extensive trips across the American landscape to see the cotton fields in the South, mechanized farms in the West, and eroded land and abandoned farms in the dustbowl states. When the film was completed, three years behind schedule, Flaherty explained his working method:

> Actually, there wasn't any story. They gave me a camera and threw me out into the field to make a film about the land and the people who live by it. I was fresh and had no preconceptions whatever; I was so sensitive you could hear me change my mind. So I merely groped my way along, photographing what seemed to me significant; it was only later that we began to see the pattern. The film is different from my others. It isn't a romance. It hasn't any specific solution for what the camera sees, but it is often critical. And that perhaps is the most amazing thing about it, that it could be made at all. It shows that democracy can face itself in the mirror without flinching. (quoted in Strauss 198)

Flaherty's assertion that he had no preconceptions should be judged in the context of the work that he and Lord and others did on various treatments of the script before shooting began. But there are several factors that help to explain what Flaherty calls the "lack of story," including his intuitive working methods, Lorentz's absence from the scenes of production, the Agriculture Department's difficulty in determining what it wanted the film to say, and the rapidly changing social situation. That Flaherty could have made *The Land* under the conditions that prevailed becomes even more "amazing."

Working for Lorentz would have been routine for a filmmaker trained in the British documentary school, but it was a relatively new experience for Flaherty. Conflicts that Flaherty experienced with Lorentz and the American bureaucracy recalled those he had had previously with Grierson and British officials in the early 1930s. Lorentz was away, committed to making *The Fight for Life,* and could not help Flaherty. Moreover, from the first Lorentz seems to have had a limited understanding of the theme and relied heavily on Flaherty's reputation for transforming documentary footage into poetic realism. In Washington, without the help of Lorentz's direct support and experience, Flaherty was frustrated by forces that inhibited his freedom to create and complete the film; traveling around the country, shooting footage, he was further hampered by Washington's demands for orderly budgets and production methods. To succeed, Flaherty would have had to be a diplomat as well as a filmmaker. Among other things, he was caught in the rivalry between the AAA and the Soil Conservation Service (SCS); the AAA subsidized farmers to keep their land out of production, while the SCS provided them with technical advice on how to get the most out of their land. The contour-plowing sequence in *The Land* is Flaherty's attempt to show the SCS viewpoint and balance the argument.[124]

The Land has a quality of rugged determination that makes it uniquely American, all the more surprising in that neither Lorentz nor Flaherty had a clear idea of what the film should say. Unlike *Nanook, Moana,* or *Man of Aran,* it could not celebrate the past. The agricultural crisis was a specific, immediate problem of national proportions, which Flaherty called "American refugees wandering in a wasteland of their own making" (quoted in Rotha, ed. Ruby 193). Seeing the spectacle of human suffering in America moved Flaherty as no subject had moved him before. However, he had to reconcile his observer's sympathy with the producer's need to provide social comment through the neat problem-solution pattern by which many traditional documentary films are made. Although Grierson generously said that *The Land* was "the greatest picture that Flaherty ever made" (quoted in Calder-Marshall 199), now, as before, Flaherty proved unable to adapt his intuitive methods to meet the social needs of the documentary film form.[125] Richard Dyer MacCann summarizes Flaherty's dilemma:

> The theme was too big for him to handle: he was not intellectually up to it, nor was his experience the sort which would have prepared him. The maker of *Nanook of the North, Moana,* and *Man of Aran* knew the long, strong commitments of simple people to the land and to ancient traditions of self-help and survival. He knew nothing of the industrial revolution. *The Land* was his own rediscovery of America and part of his slow odyssey toward some kind of self-education. (100–101)

Thus, for all Flaherty's passionate inquiry, the value of *The Land* derives not from what it says about the problem, but from what it does not say. Following is a brief synopsis of the film.[126]

II

The Land, which comprises eight basic sequences, opens with shots of a farm, farmhouse, and barn in Pennsylvania. A farm family, composed of a man and a woman with a child in her arms, suggests prosperity: "Good people of the solid old stock that settled in this country three hundred years ago." However, even in the rich farmland of Pennsylvania, the farmers are discovering the problems that come with soil erosion: "When soil fails, life fails."

The second sequence introduces the theme of farm people's relation to the soil, as Flaherty shows another farmhouse where "trouble has crept in." Erosion leads inevitably to the problems created when people are forced off their land and onto the roads in search of better soil and work. To emphasize that this problem has no geographical or racial boundaries, Flaherty records conditions in various places in the Midwest and South that have created problems for both white and black families. In a short, awkward scene, Flaherty shows an old black servant on a plantation dusting off a large bell, an action that hardly seems natural. The man, who Flaherty says "didn't seem to know that we were there," appears to be bewildered by the passing of time and the disappearance of people around him. The viewer might well question this scene for both its authenticity and necessity.

Having established the geographical and human scale of the problem, Flaherty begins the third sequence with his concern for the epic scope of the problems of the Midwestern dustbowl: "Nowhere in the world has the drama of soil erosion been played so swiftly and on so great a stage." This remark, its voice-of-god tone reminiscent of the *March of Time* series, is made all the more portentous by the musical score accompanying it. As Flaherty shows houses, farms, machinery, whole towns abandoned by the people moving westward, his narrative tone combines sentimentality and despair: "We had another name for these people once. We called them pioneers." However, in the hopeless faces of these broken people, there is little that recalls earlier pioneer settlers and their determined individualism. Wasted by circumstances and reluctant to leave their land, these outcasts are now living along the road as best they can. In attempting to create a larger context in which to understand the problem, Flaherty quotes from the Book of Job: "If my land cry against me, or that the furrows likewise thereof complain; . . . Let thistles grow instead of wheat, and cockle instead of barley." But rather than adding to our comprehension of the situation, this Biblical passage only increases the despairing tone of the narration.

The film's fourth sequence suggests a solution: the government water projects that have helped men to cultivate the western deserts. But the narrator tells us that the "magic of irrigation" benefits the owners rather than the workers, for "it wasn't their water and it isn't their land." Displaced American migrant workers, who must compete with foreigners for the chance to do hard work, are supervised by armed overseers, forced to live in filthy camps, and paid low wages. Men, women, even children are exploited by this system. The efficiency of machines has become more important than the dignity of people, who suffer to maintain subsistence.

In the fifth sequence, Flaherty both admires the machines for their size, power, and efficiency, and condemns them for their displacement of people. About a motorized cotton-picker, he says: "It doesn't pick quite clean enough yet; it is being perfected. But who can tell? One day it may be picking every boll of cotton on the world." Flaherty refuses to admit that some machines are a blessing; thus, the intent of the irony is lost as one sees the near slavelike conditions in which humans stoop to pick cotton. His comment about a bulldozer is equally ambiguous: "Multiply this monster by ten thousand; take it to some new state in the world. With such an army you could clear the ground for a great new country in no time at all." In his earlier films, Flaherty regarded human hands as the source of all craftsmanship. In *The Land,* human hands are not engaged in creation, but in the hard labor of picking crops, and they are destined to be replaced by machines that will do the work faster and cheaper. The film has moments that evoke the plight of these workers, such as the shot of a boy moving uneasily in his sleep, with his mother commenting, through Flaherty's voice, "He thinks he's picking peas."[127]

Contrasting this vision of the mechanized future with a memory of the past, there is a sentimental flashback in which a migrant worker recalls his farm in the Cumberland Mountains of Kentucky. Then, Flaherty cuts back to troubles in Iowa, where farms also fail and farmers stand in welfare lines. In a bit of direct praise for the sponsor, a man comments: "I don't know what some of us would do if it weren't for the food the government gives us."

In the next sequence, Flaherty introduces one of the most disturbing results of the overall problem: hunger. Farm prices are too low, so farmers stockpile their wheat. In images that emphasize the abundance that is locked away in ships and grain elevators, we see that America has enough grain to feed the world, but not its own starving children. The juxtaposition of shots illustrating poverty amidst plenty brings the film's presentation of the problem near to its climax. In the last two sequences, Flaherty tries to reconcile these opposing conditions.

America's agricultural abundance has been its strength in the past and will be its strength now. The "abundance in the mountains, abundance on the ranges" is emphasized in the narration and repeated in the musical theme that was first heard in the Cumberland Mountains flashback and that reminds us of the fruitful past. East and West, North and South, past and present—all are united through the soil and the people who work it.

Finally, in the concluding three-minute sequence, Flaherty presents the solutions: contour plowing, new fertilizers, and farmers' meetings. Unlike Lorentz's *The Plow that Broke the Plains* and *The River,* the emphasis here is on the people, not the government. The final scene cuts from shots of farmers at a meeting to groups of migrant workers on the road and then to the farm family that appeared in the opening shots of the film. Flaherty asserts: "The strength of a man is not great. He has not in his arms and back the colossal strength of a great machine. But a man can think. He can govern. He can plan. The great fact is the land itself and the people and the spirit of the people." The "trial draft" of Russell Lord's narration, printed in poetic form, is unified by the opening and closing emphasis on "the spirit of the people." But the narration of the film itself has paid little attention to man and his strength, and this conclusion seems to have been hastily added in an attempt to add an inspirational note to a narration characterized by a tone of almost unrelieved despair.

III

The Land marks a departure from Flaherty's earlier films. He could not look at America through the eyes of an innocent. He could not recreate life as he wanted it to be, but had to accept and record life directly as it was. Even though he yearned for the past, he could not rewrite history, restage events, or turn back the clock. The priorities of the government's task, ambiguous as they may have been, prevented him from developing some of his characteristic motifs, and the film's episodic script, based loosely on the familiar problem-solution pattern, did not permit his customary overlay of slight fictional narrative. Before making his earlier films, Flaherty had lived with members of a family until he felt that he understood them and their life in the community. In *Nanook, Moana,* and *Man of Aran,* he used these people to represent the whole community. But in *The Land,* he was looking at a national rather than a local phenomenon, which could not be represented by the plight of a single family. *The Land* is not about Flaherty's ideal family in a pre-industrial society, but about many contemporary families, uprooted from their homes and farms, victims of industrialization, poor agricultural methods, and economic chaos, wandering the roads in search of food, work, and shelter. The eyes of all he photographed, young and old alike, were mirrors of poverty, starvation, and despair.

Inevitably, *The Land* invites comparison with *The Grapes of Wrath,* both Steinbeck's novel and Ford's film. By opening and closing with the framing device of a family, Flaherty attempts to provide with a simple structural device what he was unable to provide through narration. This family—the man and the woman with a child in her arms—can only suggest the idea of the family unit; it cannot convey the magnitude or geographical scope of the problem facing them and those that they represent. Flaherty's family has neither name nor identity; in contrast, the Joad family, with its unforgettable characters, evokes an almost universal empathy. Flaherty depicts his family as victims who are barely able to accommodate their lives to the enemy of agricultural mechanization (Houston 16). Steinbeck and Ford praised the Joads' determined individualism in coping with the society that drove them off their land and onto the road; they did not so much retreat from the machines as head out, pioneer fashion, for new frontiers. Flaherty treats the farmers' problems with ambivalence, even resignation; his tone rather links *The Land* with Jean Renoir's *The Southerner* (1946), a fiction film concerned with the unpredictability of nature. However, both *The Grapes of Wrath* and *The Land* conclude with an affirmation of "the people."

The Land achieves neither the poetic realism of a typical Flaherty film, which he was not encouraged to make, nor the ideological coherence of a successful documentary film, which he was not capable of making. The issues were clear: erosion, technology displacing humans, the plight of migrant workers, surplus grain withheld from starving people. The conventional documentary film that this was intended to be would have taken an analytical view of these issues, suggesting ways to solve problems. Flaherty tried to be analytical, but he was perplexed by the magnitude of the social dilemma, and reverted, perhaps unconsciously, to yearning for the past, as in the flashback to the Cumberland Mountains farm. Both Flaherty's romantic dreams of an old Kentucky farmhouse and his realistic account of the migrant workers' camps are aspects of a larger issue which the film does not confront. Since neither Flaherty nor Lorentz seemed able to define that larger issue, it is not surprising that the film was ambivalent.

Flaherty succeeds in capturing a moment in present time but does not convey fully his understanding of its immediate problems or their relation to the future. Flaherty identifies various places in trouble around the country but also makes the crises appear larger than they actually were, thus distorting them and magnifying his sense of outrage. He suggests that the "miraculous machines" must be put to use to help people, but he offers no specific way to implement this. And by overlooking relevant considerations of time and space, he deprives his audience of important information. Officials at the Department of Agriculture tried to write an introduction that would relate the film to the contemporary crisis, but nothing came of this; in any event, very few people ever saw the film.

To a certain extent, Flaherty was the victim of rapidly changing events and his own deliberate methods: he was not able to work quickly enough to keep up with the swift evolution of American society. What he hoped to represent could only be derived from his usual, intuitive method of exploration, but that would have been too slow for the task at hand. American agriculture was changing. Within less than a decade, the government had introduced agricultural methods that had already saved many farmers; other farmers, who were dispossessed by natural and man-made disasters, had gone to work in defense industries. Nonetheless, there was considerable and lasting misfortune for the agricultural community in general—hunger, loss of land, and forced migration away from their cultural roots—a miserable situation from which American agriculture has never truly recovered. While Flaherty does not depict either the extent of these changes or the speed with which they occurred, he does praise American strengths in a time of national crisis and impending international war and takes a courageous stand against the human suffering brought by technological progress: "We are wasting more than our land, we are wasting our promise as a people, as a nation."

IV

The principal strengths of *The Land* are its cinematography and editing. Flaherty had previously kept his camera still, but he sometimes re-framed shots, or used pan and tilt shots when absolutely necessary to keep the subject in frame. But here the dominant visual style of the film is the moving camera, which not only reflects the questioning tone of the narration, but also captures the restless mood of the country. His ceaseless moving, turning, circling, and looking back says more than he does in words. Deep-focus cinematography was evident in American nonfiction film as early as *The River* (1937), and Flaherty's use of it reflects his nostalgic attitude (Weaver 21). Some of his visual imagery recalls the work of the great documentary photographers of the 1930s, Walker Evans and Dorothea Lange among them, whose stark images first reflected the human plight of the depression years. Inevitably, *The Land* further recalls imagery in Lorentz's earlier films, *The Plow that Broke the Plains* (with cinematography by Paul Strand, Ralph Steiner, and Leo Hurwitz) and *The River* (Floyd Crosby, Stacy Woodward, and Willard Van Dyke).[128]

Flaherty's assistants, all cameramen accustomed to shooting standard documentary footage, were Floyd Crosby (with whom he shot *Tabu*), Irving Lerner, Arthur Rothstein, Douglas Baker, and Charles Herbert (only Flaherty, Lerner, and Crosby are listed in the credits).[129] They were trained to use conventional methods and equipment, to shoot from a script, and to provide footage that an editor could cut in conformity with that script. Flaherty, however, worked intuitively, using his eye instead of an exposure meter, shooting what looked or felt right instead of following a script. Thus, they returned from their twenty-five-thousand mile exploration of the United States with seventy-five-thousand feet of exposed footage. Irving Lerner said that Flaherty "did not want to have anything to do with an exposure-meter or anything else that did not rely on intuition and experience" (quoted in Rotha, ed. Ruby 194). While working on the film, Flaherty admitted to Lerner that he had "never tackled a tougher or more confusing job and there are times when I don't know whether I am standing on my head or not" (quoted in Rotha, ed. Ruby 197).

How tough or confusing this job was could best be judged by Helen Van Dongen, one of the most gifted, creative, skilled editors in nonfiction film history, who completed *The Land*. Called in to work virtually alone after the entire film was shot, and working with Flaherty for the first time, she recalls Flaherty's groans at screenings: "My God, what are we going to do with all this stuff?"[130] Van Dongen had to meet the difficult challenges of working with a sensitive artist who resisted professional assistance, of developing a visual point-of-view to unify the miles of random footage, and of providing an overall structure for the film. She did what she could to edit the massive amounts of uncatalogued footage, to shape its sweeping contours into something more than a cry of anguish, but there is only so much that even a gifted editor can do with the sort of material Flaherty provided. In retrospect, Van Dongen said: "I don't think *The Land* has anything which is particularly mine. There are certain indications of my style, but the film scatters over too many things to have time to develop" (quoted in Achtenberg 54). While she gave some structure and coherence to the film, there were so many problems from conception, through production, to

Flaherty and Helen Van Dongen during a break from an
editing session (Van Dongen wears white cotton editing
gloves).

completion, that, even if Flaherty and Van Dongen had worked together
from the beginning, it is doubtful that they would have achieved more. Van
Dongen understood the film's problem-solution pattern as a classic documentary structure, but it was not surprising that she had difficulty in
achieving the necessary relationship between the two elements, since Flaherty faced the same obstacle in the script. Yet, even though Flaherty's
unplanned shooting created so many problems for her, she later praised his
intuitive and sensitive eye for shooting authentic, unrehearsed events.[131]
Considering their differences—in experience and temperament—it is remarkable that Van Dongen and Flaherty were able to complete *The Land*,
to remain friends, and to work together again on *Louisiana Story*.

The original scenario for *The Land*, based on Russell Lord's book *Behold
Our Land* (1938), which Flaherty helped Lord to adapt for the screen,[132]
demonstrates far more narrative control and overall unity than does the

completed film. As we have seen, Flaherty had, as usual, resisted using another person's preconceived script and set out with camera and crew to find the story in the American countryside.[133] Although, ultimately, Flaherty did use much of Lord's scenario in his narration, he made substantial cuts, commenting that "colorful words—words that throw pictures—get in the way of the picture" (quoted in Lord, *Forever the Land* 28). As a realist, Flaherty always relied more on cinematography than on narration or editing, and he thought of *The Land* in terms of a silent film.[134] As a result, in editing the film, Helen Van Dongen had difficulty resolving the conflict between the sight and sound images, which might have been less of a problem had Flaherty shot the film along the lines of Lord's original script. By repeating certain shots, Van Dongen underscored the prevalence of certain problems, but repetition itself could not correct the structural imbalance of the film. In an attempt to make some order out of chaos, the last sequence is composed almost entirely of shots already used in the film; this effort to capitalize on their cumulative force is undercut by the narration, which, at the end, lacks almost all ability to convince.

In the late 1930s and early 1940s, the narration of American nonfiction film often had a characteristically "American" sound. This is evident in the influence of Walt Whitman on Pare Lorentz's text for *The River*—a text that James Joyce said was "the most beautiful prose I have heard in ten years" (quoted in White 10). To a lesser degree, Whitman's influence can be heard in Russell Lord's text for *The Land*. Helen Van Dongen convinced Flaherty to increase his personal commitment to the film by reading the narration, much as she had convinced Ernest Hemingway to speak the narration that he wrote for another film she edited, Joris Ivens's *The Spanish Earth* (1937). The first-person plural narrative effectively involves the viewer ("We came to a town . . ." or "We came upon a scene . . ."). Flaherty's flinty voice suits the expressionless faces of the people on the screen, and he shows deep concern for them as well as a brief wistfulness for the "old ways" he likes so much.

The "American influence" can also be heard in the music used for nonfiction films of the period, especially that of Virgil Thomson *(The Plow that Broke the Plains, The River,* and *Louisiana Story)*, Aaron Copland *(The City* and *The Cummington Story)*, Douglas Moore *(Power and the Land)*, and Marc Blitzstein *(Native Land)*. Richard Arnell composed the musical score for *The Land,* and described it variously as being "uncompromisingly . . . contrapuntal" (12) and "rather like a Purcell fantasia" (quoted in Rotha, ed. Ruby 204). It was Arnell's first film as a composer (although he had earlier made several 16mm films himself), and he was recommended for the work by Virgil Thomson, a master at musical scoring for nonfiction film. Arnell admired Flaherty's work and was eager to work with him, but, like many others who had worked with Flaherty, Arnell was confused by his working methods. That Arnell's score is not a success can perhaps be attributed both to his lack of experience in the work and Flaherty's overall problems with completing the film. In his score for *Louisiana Story,* Thomson created musical themes that successfully reconciled technology and nature. In *The Land,* no such reconciliation seems possible (either in the narration, narrative structure, or musical score), and Arnell's insistent, dramatic music tends to overwhelm the images that it accompanies.[135] To express the dual ideas of hope and energy in the film's ending, Arnell wrote a fugue, which he believed would bring the film to a logical conclusion (Arnell 13; Rotha, ed. Ruby 204–205). If Arnell had juxtaposed motif against motif, problem against solution, perhaps this counterpoint would have given the film the ending it needs; however, by itself, it cannot infuse the ending with logic or unity. As it is, what unity the *The Land* has derives from the good intentions of its director, editor, and musical composer, but not from its ideas, either verbal or musical.

V

In April 1942, five months after the United States declared war on Japan, *The Land* was released for a brief period and then withdrawn from general distribution to prevent its use by the enemy in anti-American propaganda films.[136] Thus, at the time, few people saw it, and critical opinion was divided (Murphy 76). In succeeding years, we have recognized that *The Land* was produced by a complex and not altogether complementary set of factors: Flaherty's return to the United States; his passionate expression of sympathy for a social problem he could only begin to comprehend; and his "belated attempt to come to terms with the twentieth century" (Corliss 237). People conscious of the environment, particularly in the emerging and developing nations, still confront the same issues that Flaherty addressed in *The Land.* Now, as then, it is not easy to understand them or to sort them out precisely.

The Land was a puzzle to its creators from its conception to its completion. The depth of the American agricultural and human misfortune daunted them, and neither Lorentz, as producer, nor Flaherty, as director, was able to hold a consistent viewpoint in treating its large themes. The historical roots and international significance of the problem also eluded them. They neither knew what they wanted to say or how to say it. While arbitrariness about style was always Flaherty's enemy, it is nowhere more apparent than in *The Land*. Ironically, he resisted compromise with the documentary style and then seemed to abandon not only his own style, but also his traditionally humanistic viewpoint. In *The Land*, he seemed ambivalent about the condition of man, the subject that is at the heart of his previous work. Russell Lord's original scenario began with lines that Flaherty rejected: "This is a picture of American soil and of all things living which grow out of it—especially Man." In the film's final minutes, Flaherty asks: "What about the people?" Had he asked that question in the beginning, he might have been able to provide the answer, for he knew it all along: the human spirit prevails.

VI

When the United States entered the Second World War, independent and Hollywood studio filmmakers began the rapid production of information, training, military, and propaganda films. Flaherty was only briefly involved in the effort, because he could not produce a film on a schedule that would preserve the timeliness of its issues, and because he had neither the temperament nor the training to make a film based on another person's ideas. In 1942, Frank Capra assigned Flaherty to a newsreel project, as part of the activities of the Motion Picture Bureau of the Office of War Information, but soon had to let him go. Other great directors were able to adapt, to work quickly, and to complete vital projects—among them, John Huston, William Wyler, Walt Disney, John Ford—but, as Richard Griffith believes, Flaherty "sabotaged himself" by refusing to compromise his methods (quoted in Rotha, ed. Ruby 230). At issue was not Flaherty's patriotism, but his ability to undertake and complete the work involved.

Thus, *The Land*, Robert Flaherty's tribute to the strength of the American people, can be regarded as his war film, what Van Dongen called his "badge of courage" ("Robert J. Flaherty" 220). It was the first film in which Flaherty confronted the economic, sociological, and technological problems of his time, declaring personal war on the technology that changed American agriculture and resulted in hunger and unemployment in the world's richest country. *The Land*, which is about the enemy within, not the enemy overseas, reveals much about the filmmaker himself. Flaherty was both elated and depressed by the problems he encountered in his travels across America, and certainly he was confused by the challenges he faced in completing this film. He believed in the subject but not the style; he shot footage with conviction but not with purpose; he had something to say, but he did not know how to organize his argument. *The Land* was honest and simple, and if Flaherty had been able to join his social insight to social comment, he might have produced a very powerful and influential film. What redeems *The Land* is not the neat solution to problems that the social documentary film is supposed to provide, but rather the haunting images of America's poor and suffering people. It falls short of reaching Griersonian ideals, but it succeeds as a Robert Flaherty film, as a work of keen insight, rugged determination, and visual beauty.

CHAPTER EIGHT

Louisiana Story (1948)

Memory, Myth, and Actuality

I

As a filmmaker, Robert Flaherty had virtually nothing to do during the Second World War. The American film industry was almost totally engaged in the production of official war films, to which Flaherty was unable to adapt his methods, and there was little money available for the production of independent nonfiction films.[137] According to Richard Griffith, Flaherty was "wholly out of tune with the mood of the country and most people" during this period (quoted in Rotha, ed. Ruby 230), suffering what Rotha called "the unhappiest period of frustration in his whole life" (230). When, unknown and inexperienced, he had begun his career as a filmmaker shortly after the end of World War I, he obtained Revillon Frères' support for the expedition that resulted in *Nanook*. In 1943, on the twenty-first anniversary of *Nanook*, *New Movies* published a special issue of tribute. Now, world famous and revered, Flaherty could not find work as a filmmaker, and even more significant, seems not to have had any plans to make films.

In the midst of this despair, when it looked as if he might never make another film, he was presented with the opportunity of a filmmaker's lifetime. In 1944, toward the end of World War II, the Standard Oil Company of New Jersey (now Exxon Corporation) approached him with a contract to make the film that became *Louisiana Story*. Thus, both Flaherty's first and last films were sponsored by companies that had the faith to permit him to make films his own way, and it is perhaps not coincidental that *Nanook* and *Louisiana Story* are his best films.

Standard Oil wanted Flaherty to make a film that would convey to the public the difficulty and danger involved in the exploration for oil—not an ordinary documentary or industrial film, but one good enough to be booked into commercial theaters. The company did not want a film about itself (Standard Oil is mentioned only briefly in a credit title thanking its employees on the drilling rig), but rather one that would enhance the overall image of the oil industry. It would explain to oil company share-holders the reasons for risking capital in oil exploration, show environmen-talists that the industry was concerned both with exploring and with respecting natural resources, and, moreover, accomplish these goals by demonstrating industrial support for the arts. In his planning, Flaherty took into account his sponsor's desire for a film that would show the difficulties and risks involved in getting oil out of the ground. However, in making the film, Flaherty, as usual, relied upon his own imagination.

The contract, unprecedented in the history of the nonfiction film, not only reflected the patron's generosity, but also guaranteed the artist's free-dom.[138] The company agreed to pay all the costs of the film's production (the total reached $258,000), to turn over all the theater revenue to Fla-herty, and, most remarkable of all, to give him complete artistic control (Barnouw, *Documentary* 216–21). However, Standard Oil's generosity also reflected good business practice: years before corporations underwrote the arts as generously as they do today, their management recognized the power and value of imaginative public relations. In any event, Standard Oil seems to have been satisfied that its money was well-invested in achieving the many objectives they had set for the film, and aside from some critics' confusion over Flaherty's attitude toward industry, the film was not unduly criticized, as it would undoubtedly be today, for its corporate sponsorship.

Louisiana Story, Flaherty's most ambitious and most beautiful film, is made out of myth, memory, and actuality. It culminates his career by recapitulating the central motifs and philosophy of the films that preceded it. In *Nanook, Moana,* and *Man of Aran,* Flaherty portrayed life free from industrialization, and in *Industrial Britain* and *The Land,* he considered the effects of technology on manual labor. In *Louisiana Story,* with industry as the sponsor, he represented industrialization as neither threatening nor beneficent, but instead created a rich ambiguity of meaning in depicting the coming of the oil industry to the Louisiana bayou. Flaherty, acknowledg-ing the film's dreamlike mood, called its narrative a "fantasy," but in presenting a world out of time—a world that does not refer in any way to America after World War II—he is also offering a world out of mind, the autobiography of a romantic who, at the age of sixty-two, retained the wonder of a boy exploring the world around him.

In his travels, Flaherty met various people who became characters in his films—among them, Nanook, Moana, and Tiger-King; this film, however,

Flaherty during the making of *Louisiana Story*.

presents a portrait of himself and of the Cajun boy who serves as his persona. Frances Flaherty said:

> *Louisiana Story* is autobiography. It is Bob remembering his childhood with his father, a mining engineer, on the Canadian frontier searching in the earth not for "black gold," that is, oil, but for the true shining golden metal itself. The wonder of this world in the mind and heart of a boy is the truth of the film and its enchantment." *(Odyssey* 38)

Flaherty sees this world through the eyes of Alexander Napoleon Ulysses Latour (the fancifully allusive name that he gave to the character played by Joseph Boudreaux), and evident throughout is a rapport between the director and this winsome youth that recalls not only Flaherty's collaboration with Nanook and Moana, but also his affectionate relationships with Mikeleen and Sabu.[139]

The principal characters of both *Nanook* and *Louisiana Story* are explorers: Nanook (the father) and Alexander (the son). Here, Flaherty records and celebrates the boy, who, through his innocence, curiosity, superstition, and powers of magic, seems, in Wordworth's sense, the father of the men who come to the bayou in search of oil. He is there before they arrive, amused by their behavior while they are working there, and remains after they leave. The bayou provides his experience and circumscribes his life, and even though he might have been spoiled by contact with the world outside, the impression left at the film's conclusion is that his innocence has, if anything, been confirmed.

Thus, in *Louisiana Story,* Robert Flaherty met a challenge that had bested him in making *The Land:* the reconciliation of opposing forces. On the mythic level, he succeeded in reconciling the opposite worlds of the boy and the men, the alligator and the oil derrick; on the personal level, the integrity of the independent filmmaker was reconciled with the needs of the industrial sponsor, his views with those of his collaborators. It had taken Flaherty a lifetime of exploring his own artistry to reach this point, and he brought to its production everything that he had learned.

In one important aspect, this film was different from any previous film Flaherty had made. He chose an impressive group of artists with whom to work as his collaborators, including Richard Leacock, the cinematographer; Helen Van Dongen, the editor, who also served as associate producer; and Virgil Thomson, who wrote the musical score. Flaherty's wife Frances worked with him on the story. They were not asked to join him midway, to help solve a problem (as Helen Van Dongen was asked to join him on *The Land),* but, rather, were with Flaherty from the beginning through the completion of the film.

Although all of them helped Flaherty bring *Louisiana Story* to completion, it is without a doubt that Helen Van Dongen played the most important role by giving the film its clarity, coherence, structure, and rhythm. In "Three Hundred and Fifty Cans of Film," an account of her work with Flaherty on this project, she wrote:

> The editor working with a great director can do no better than discover and disclose the director's design. When an editor is working for a confused

director, that of course is another matter. The editor is a *member of a team*, working in close contact with the director. The director is the central figure, who through creative direction of actors, camera and editing, gives shape and meaning to the story, and is ultimately responsible for the form and content of the film. (57–58)

Here, Van Dongen describes an ideally balanced relationship between film director and editor. However, the actual creative climate in which *Louisiana Story* was made was different. Her production diary and articles on the editing of the film, read in the context of other accounts, suggest an atmosphere of confusion and, at times, chaos, with apparently little of the "close contact" she mentions above.[140] In the middle of editing the film, she wrote of her isolation from Flaherty: "This is one of the hardest parts of this job. Never a discussion, never an exchange of ideas about incongruities or possibilities or form, for that matter" (quoted in Rotha, ed. Ruby 243). As associate producer, as well as editor, Van Dongen played a major role in planning and shaping the film, and the disagreements generally had to do with planning the shooting so that the footage could then be assembled in some coherent way. As always, Flaherty observed life closely, following the dictates of his intuition and imagination as he prepared the narrative, but he disregarded the narrative when he got behind the camera and, according to Richard Leacock, followed his usual method of shooting everything that seemed even remotely relevant to the idea he had in mind (Levin 210–11). As a result, Van Dongen had what she called "collisions" with Robert and Frances Flaherty, but Flaherty realized that, even though they disagreed on many points, he could not complete the film without her. Rotha (ed. Ruby) says that the spontaneity and naturalism of Flaherty's casual method of shooting remained a problem for the editor, but, in spite of that, "Van Dongen's assembling of the footage as shooting proceeded was a more integral part of the film's construction than in any previous Flaherty film" (241).

With *Louisiana Story,* Flaherty and his associates had to reach several goals: to record the mysterious wilderness of the bayous as yet untouched by industrial civilization; to maintain the lyrical tone established in the opening sequence and make it appropriate to the overall narrative; and to meet the needs of their sponsor. Moreover, they had to sustain an acceptable point-of-view; writing in "Robert J. Flaherty: 1884–1951," Van Dongen made an insightful observation about this:

It was often said that Flaherty was naive and looked upon the world with the innocent eyes of a child. It takes great sophistication to portray a world of one's own making, then to display it seen by a child. His mind was not as

> innocent as a child's, nor was he naive. He had a penetrating mind and acute powers of observation. He was fully aware of the miseries, struggles, and ugliness of the world, but these embarrassed him. Whatever he thought of it in the privacy of his thinking, he was unwilling to display these thoughts publicly. He averted his eye and his camera from trouble and sorrow and bitterness, chose instead situations where man could still meet a not too complex challenge. Be it tattooing to prove manhood or the hunt to stay alive (at least temporarily), his hero would come off the victor. . . . His films were not the statements of the historian. With *Louisiana Story* Flaherty drops all pretense, confesses that he helped nature along sometimes, and admits freely that it is all a fable. (226–28)

Flaherty had a simple view of the world, but he was not innocent. As his other films demonstrate, Flaherty did not wholeheartedly espouse Standard Oil's message: he knew that men could spoil, even destroy, the natural environment, that innocence was virtually meaningless against the material strength of the industrial world, and that human beings paid dearly for the benefits provided by technology. Flaherty also knew that his film would be worthless if the sponsor's message took precedence over those values that characterized his other films. Yet he could not wholly ignore his sponsor's reason for making this film. Thus, he made the best choice possible under the circumstances and narrated the film through the viewpoint of a boy who is so close to nature that his only friend is a gentle raccoon and who will fight the alligator he believes destroyed that friend. This proved to be a brilliant decision for the film; it not only provided a persona to serve as Flaherty's advocate, but also preserved the wondrous spirit of boyhood that is among its most enduring qualities.

Following is a brief synopsis of *Louisiana Story,* divided for purposes of discussion into six sequences.

II

Louisiana Story begins slowly with images that quietly convey the primeval beauty and mysterious mood of the Petit Anse bayou: lotus leaves, tiny bugs skimming over the water surface, an alligator floating lazily, white clouds reflected in the water, dew drops, magnificent birds, tree trunks in the dark water, silvery Spanish moss hanging from the branches. As we first see Alexander Napoleon Ulysses Latour and his pet raccoon in a canoe, the narrator (Flaherty himself) introduces the boy, telling us about his belief in mermaids and werewolves, his ever-present bag of salt, and the "little something he carries inside his shirt" (which we later discover is a frog), his talisman against werewolves.[141] Alexander is ready to shoot a porcupine when he hears two explosions, his first awareness of something foreign. The aural images that follow suggest the size and power of some anonymous monster, like the superstitions and spirits in which he believes, but we do not actually see any menacing threat.

Later, we see his father signing a contract with the oil company agent and realize that the bayou will never be the same again, for already speeding boats are cutting through the quiet waters, making noise and waves. Virgil Thomson's score introduces a lyrical theme for the boy, but it is shortly overwhelmed by the roar of the company's speedboats and later by the sounds of ceaseless drilling. The Latour family seems ambivalent toward this activity, neither hostile to the invasion, nor hopeful of overnight riches. But Alexander realizes what is going to happen when, after his canoe is swamped in the wake of a speeding boat, he sees the surveying team mark a location for drilling with a stake in the water. This stake, a recurrent symbol of their invasion, is first surrounded by the debris pulled down the river by the drilling barges, then replaced by the derrick, and finally by the so-called "Christmas tree" or pumping unit that controls the flow of oil into the pipelines. The oil derrick is equally effective as a symbol, a steel structure that Flaherty invests with an abstract force and almost spiritual grandeur. Alexander's first sight of it is unforgettable. Gliding through the grassy marshes on an unseen barge, it towers clean and powerful over the surrounding flatlands.[142] This juxtaposition of scenic environment with alien technology, underscored by a majestic musical theme, and perceived by Alexander with a certain neutrality, creates the ambiguity of meaning for which realist cinema strives. The awesome and foreboding phenomenon is observed, but not explained; moving, but apparently unmanned; beautiful by the standards of industry, but ugly in contrast to the bayou's natural beauty. This first sequence establishes mood, character, and conflict, and, until this point, the theme is of secondary importance. Each image advances these elements and strengthens our understanding of the prevailing mood and empathy with the emotional atmosphere. We witness what appears to be the corruption of the boy's paradise, and, like Flaherty and the boy, are unable to do anything but observe.

The realist style of this first sequence is continued in the brief second sequence. While the men are fishing from the drilling barge, catching only little fish, Alexander arrives in his canoe and proudly displays the big fish he has caught. Gently suggesting that it is luck, not bait, that catches fish, he spits on his hook and catches another big fish right in front of them. The simple charm of this simulation makes this as believable a fishing story as any other. The men, who are charmed by his simple ways, invite him on board, but Alexander rejects the invitation and departs.

The third sequence is composed in a more formal style that emphasizes the complex oil-drilling operation. The editing of this sequence, referred to by Van Dongen as the "ballet of the roughnecks," depends on the contrapuntal interplay between sound and picture images.[143] Even though Flaherty used sound in all of his films except *Nanook* and *Moana* (both made before sound was introduced to motion pictures), he never really understood it as a formal property of cinematic realism.[144] In this third sequence of *Louisiana Story,* there is a sophisticated soundtrack, composed of sounds, general and specific, each with its own characteristics, recorded at the site.[145]

Frequent cuts from the boy's boat to the derrick further emphasize the contrast between the placid rhythms of his world and the purely formalistic movements of the machinery. Here the beauty of the photography, much of which Flaherty and Leacock shot at night, is matched by Van Dongen's detailed cinematic explanation and evocation of the industrial process. The drilling is seen from many angles—from the front, from above, through the men's eyes, and through the boy's. Once inside the derrick housing, Alexander becomes friendly with the workmen and tells them about his magic—his bag of salt and the "something else" hidden in his shirt and brought out to frighten "them" (the werewolves). The formal beauty of this sequence occupies the viewer's complete attention, and the emotional quality is sustained through our admiration of the men's skill with their machines; the sense of danger inherent in their working with rapidly coiling and uncoiling chains that could easily cause severe injury; the boy's awe for this unknown world of technology; and the magic implicit in the men's belief in their technology and explicit in the boy's belief in his talismans.

The boy's reference to "them" (now, apparently, real alligators instead of mythical werewolves) provides the transition between the third and fourth sequences. Having established Alexander's firsthand observation of the derrick and drilling operation, Flaherty begins the fourth sequence with a distinct change in setting and mood. Here the boy is alone in nature, its kindly aspects symbolized by his pet raccoon, its evil forces by an alligator. After drifting for a while in his canoe, he ties his raccoon to the boat and the boat to a tree, and sets out to explore the shore. Finding a nest of newly-hatched alligators, he holds one in his hand; watching him from the water, the mother crawls from the water onto the bank and moves stealthily toward the boy. As the music heightens the suspense of a moment that could become tragic, the alligator makes a warning sound, the boy runs back to safety, and the scene ends. Once again, the boy is calm and full of wonder as he contemplates the life held in his hand, a life as mysterious and (by extension through the mother alligator) as dangerous as the life and activity he observed on the derrick. In the film (but not always in actual bayou life), the alligator is man's real enemy—primeval, vicious, and destructive.[146] Later, we realize that oil and the drilling operation may merit the same description.

Meanwhile, the raccoon has broken its tether and left the boat. Van Dongen juxtaposes shots of the swimming raccoon with shots of an alligator that has just attacked an egret; this deliberately suggests that the alligator is also in pursuit of the raccoon, which seems to be swimming for its life. The boy's premonition that his pet has been lost can be felt by anyone who has lost a pet and sought for it in vain. In an act of revenge that is more bold than believable, Alexander traps an alligator (first having spit on the huge hook), fights it in a tug-of-war, but loses. He calls out to his father, who is searching for the boy and runs to help, and soon after, we see Alexander with the alligator's skin, victoriously flexing his muscles.[147] The shot/reverse shot montage captures all the excitement and danger of an event that we never wholly see on the screen, but only experience in the imagination: the boy on one end of a slim rope and the alligator, with a hook through its jaw, on the other. Although it appears to have been staged and hardly seems believable, the actual fight was covered by two cameras, with additional footage of a struggling alligator photographed in a wildlife refuge. The difficulty of intercutting this additional footage with that of the actual fight contributes to the impression that the fight was staged.[148]

The focus of the penultimate sequence of the film is, again, the oil-drilling operation. Mr. Latour, Alexander's father, teases the workmen about their failure to strike oil; ironically, this scene is followed by a wildcat blowout at the derrick. There is a tremendous rush of gas and salt water, followed by shots of newspaper headlines that document the event, a device that was a cinematic cliché even before Pare Lorentz exhausted what remained of its vitality in *The River* (1937). Mr. Latour warns Alexander to stay away from "that hole," saying "it's no place for a boy now." However, the technique of slant drilling eventually solves the problems created by the blowout, and the well comes gushing in. Again Flaherty establishes the scene's potential for ambiguity. The dangerous blowout, which eventually leads to a successful capping of the well, undercuts the father's skepticism and suggests that his old ways and gentle habits will be a thing of the past now that the efficient younger workmen have proven that they know what they are doing. Perhaps the audience concurs with this resolution of a conflict that seems so simple and inevitable. But Alexander regards the blowout as nature's revenge against the men, who earlier laughed at his offer to help them with his magic. Bewildered and hurt by their laughter, he nonetheless drops his bag of salt down the shaft and spits after it. He believes in this magic, not in oil, and he wants to prove himself against the strange and so-far unsuccessful attempts of the men and their machines. This stage in Alexander's rite of initiation is explicit as he invokes the world of the *other*—his salt, spit, and spirits—to call forth from the unpredictable earth the oil that has drawn the men to the bayou and the boy to the men. The development of the film's motifs approaches a climax in the juxtaposition of tranquility and disruption, superstition and technology, skepticism and confidence, youth and age, nature and man's harnessing of its forces.

The final sequence of *Louisiana Story* is both its most evocative and its weakest. Mr. Latour returns from the city not only with the standard provisions, but also with presents, a dress and double-boiler for his wife and a rifle for his son.[149] A display of drying skins suggests that Mr. Latour has made his living as a trapper, and it seems apparent that their new wealth will not affect their material way of life and that they will continue to live in their little cabin. To show Latour's simple ways, Flaherty adopts another cinematic cliché and has him write a letter to the oil company agent ("Dear Friend") telling him what he already knows: that the work has been completed.[150] Alexander goes outside to test the gun, and he sees his raccoon for the first time since he presumed that it had been killed by the alligator that he, in turn, killed. This happy reunion serves to round out the narrative structure. The drilling barge leaves as quietly as it arrived, the water is calm once again, the boy has a new gun (to replace his rusty old one), and his pet raccoon is back at his side.

Even if oil and money have not changed the Latours' way of living, life itself has nonetheless changed in the bayou. The wooden stake has been replaced by the pumping unit; the family is aware of the increased value of its property; and Alexander is aware of an industrial power beyond the already powerful worlds of nature and his imagination. The boy paddles his canoe out to the pipe sprouting from the water, climbs to the top, and in a final gesture, waves goodbye to the departing men as he spits into the water. The spitting confirms his belief that his magic, not technology, brought in the well. However, since spitting is also an age-old gesture of contempt, it may represent the boy's scorn for the noise and confusion of the drilling, for the men's laughter at his belief in magic. It may be Flaherty's contempt as well, his last comment on the machines that he hated so much. Although Flaherty is not contemptuous of the company that sponsored his film, through his persona, he spits, smiles, and says good riddance to all industrial forces. This final scene, complete with its evocative symbols (rifle, raccoon, spitting, pumping unit), concludes with a shot of the boy that recalls the film's opening. Sitting astride an alien complex of pipes, this shy and awkward lad, named after conquerors of history and myth, remains the hero of all that he surveys.[151]

III

Louisiana Story served both the practical needs of Standard Oil and the poetic spirit of Robert Flaherty. Out of materials that might otherwise have become a prosaic industrial film, Flaherty made a dramatic film showing the difficulty and the danger involved in the discovery of oil. To all members of his audience—stockholders, environmentalists, schoolchildren, and the general public—the film explained not only the process by which oil was discovered in the bayou, but also confirmed something of the mystery of nature. It told the story of men—the hardworking, experienced younger men on the drilling rig; the older, skeptical Mr. Latour—and, through the eyes of a boy, it created a special world, haunted by werewolves and mermaids. The film is a study in contrasts between technology and superstition, men and boys, the bayou and the world beyond, and success and failure. The noise and power of technology, developed so beautifully in the sequence known as the "Ballet of the Roughnecks," are contrasted with the beautiful, quiet, and lyrical scenes depicting Alexander in the bayou, exploring, watching, listening, or fishing.

Flaherty had been free to indulge himself and his view of the world. Not only did he have a contract that ensured him complete artistic freedom, and collaborators who would help him realize his vision, but he had conceived the brilliant idea of revealing his story through the eyes and thoughts of a boy. Alexander Napoleon Ulysses Latour was not a one-dimensional character like Mikeleen or Sabu, but a real boy, living in a world of reality, myth, and memory, and it is no wonder that Flaherty took such care in directing the boy who played him. Flaherty's wonder and curiosity about life become Alexander's and thus become ours. The film is a fable, both simple and complex, raising more questions than it answers and using both subconscious symbols and newspaper headlines to reveal actuality. Today, when oil is both a natural and a political resource, treasured by virtue of its scarcity and value, the film gains new worth, tantalizing us with the precious, mysterious balance that exists between man and nature in an imaginary world without politics.

In *Louisiana Story*, there is realism in Flaherty's treatment of the oil industry, but also poetry in his love of nature and elegy in his celebration of innocence. From its beginning in the dreamlike images and the narrative tone set by Flaherty's voice, through the formal structure of the oil drilling sequence, to the conclusion, *Louisiana Story* is a soft, lyrical film whose images linger in the memory. The six sequences unfold leisurely; the first engages the viewer with images of mysterious shapes and shadows, and the others tell the chronological narrative. Circular in construction, the film moves from peace and quiet to activity and noise and finally back to peace and quiet. The crew enters the isolated bayou, drills for a well, establishes a pumping unit, and then departs. The boy is there at the beginning and ending of the film; although the central section concentrates on the industrial operation, his view of the world is not changed, but rather confirmed, by the activity. The fundamental aim of this narrative is to express the feeling and atmosphere of the place, not just the actuality of the situation.

As had happened before in his career, Flaherty realized that he had a problem in attempting to discover a narrative within nature and letting that narrative reveal itself. Although he had the overall concept, and had no difficulty in translating the moods he wanted into expressive visual images, the larger design would have eluded him without the contributions of his collaborators in scenario, photography, editing, and music. Thus, the film's beauty is partly a result of Flaherty's insistence on many of his traditional ways of working, and partly a product of his collaborative experiments with cinematography, particularly with the synchronous sound camera. He was agreeable to the overall use of sound, and, for the first time, directed scenes with dialogue.

From the beginning, it was clear that Virgil Thomson's musical score would play an integral part in *Louisiana Story*. Thomson and Van Dongen planned in detail how its themes would develop character and narrative and would function with the intricate sound track.[152] Thomson, pleased to work with Flaherty, found the director to be "patient, fearless, and trusting of himself," without the "self-doubt" that he found in Pare Lorentz when they had worked together earlier on *The River* (393). He wrote:

> *Louisiana Story*'s music is of three kinds—folk music, scenery music, and noise-music. The Cajun people are represented by their waltzes and square dances and the tunes of the songs they sing. Natural scenery is depicted through musical devices adapted from Mendelssohn, Debussy, and other landscape composers. The noise-music used is the recorded sound of the oil-well-drilling machinery. I call it music because, as compounded and shaped by Helen Van Dongen into a rich and deafening accompaniment for a passage of well digging one whole reel (nine minutes) long, these noises make a composition. Also, I find this composition more interesting to follow

than almost any of the industrial evocations, including my own, that musicians have composed with tonal materials. (394)

Thomson was awarded the 1949 Pulitzer Prize for the music, the first time this prize had been given for a film score.[153] *Louisiana Story* was generally well received by the critics, was named by the National Board of Review of Motion Pictures as one of the ten best films of 1948, and in 1949 was awarded the Order of St. George at the Venice Film Festival (Murphy 78–81).

IV

The achievement of *Louisiana Story* suggests that Flaherty-as-auteur was more successful when working with artists such as Leacock, Van Dongen, and Thomson than when working alone.[154] All were masters of a particular craft, and each was encouraged to contribute as much as possible to the film without imposing their own imaginative conceptions on the director's vision. They helped Flaherty to discover within actuality those elements that would realize the contours of that vision, and, moreover, they helped him to disclose them through cinematic language. During the making of the film, Flaherty repeated his familiar remark: "A film is the longest distance between two points" (quoted differently in Rotha, ed. Ruby 5, 239). He also remarked to Van Dongen that "the art of the motion picture is the art of exclusion," sometimes quoted as: "The making of a film is the elimination of the non-essential."[155] Although he rarely expressed his aesthetics of film, that simple truth reveals much of what he had learned from a lifetime of filmmaking, including what he had learned on *Louisiana Story* in working so closely and so well with his fellow artists.[156]

In Robert Flaherty's *oeuvre, Louisiana Story* stands alone as a small masterpiece—lyric, poetic, humanistic; as a realistic account of a major industrial process; and as a romantic elegy to a world that Flaherty envisioned and illuminated more completely here than in any of his other films. He had never before made a more ambitious film than *Louisiana Story,* and, despite its success and his subsequent involvement in several filmmaking projects, it was his last film. In 1948, he made plans for a film on Picasso's *Guernica,* then in the Museum of Modern Art in New York City. This was a formidable challenge, an attempt to render the fervor of Picasso's antiwar painting in cinematic terms, but he did not complete the experiment, although a short, silent version of this otherwise unfinished film was released. In 1939, German filmmaker Curt Oertel had made *Michelangelo,* a documentary based on the life of Michelangelo, and considered to be an artistic success. After World War II, it was held by the United States as enemy property, and various filmmakers—including Flaherty, John Grierson, Helen Van Dongen, and others—were asked to re-edit it, primarily to shorten it and improve the soundtrack. They all refused to edit another artist's work, but Flaherty agreed to the use of his name as producer in the United States release of the film as *The Titan* in 1950. In 1951, Flaherty entered into a similar agreement with the film *St. Matthew Passion*.[157]

In the same year, he formed Robert Flaherty Film Associates, his own company designed for the production of institutional and public relations films, but this organization never actually made any films. In 1950, he went to Germany, where, as a cultural ambassador for the U.S. Department of State, he had a great success in showing and discussing a selection of his films. At this time, Flaherty made plans for a film on the split between West and East Germany (to be titled *The Green Border*), as well as a film on racial integration in Hawaii (to be titled *East is West*); he proposed both projects to the State Department, and although there was some interest in them, neither was realized.

In 1951, Flaherty was honored by the Screen Directors Guild with a retrospective showing of his films at the Museum of Modern Art. Because Flaherty needed to work as an artist as well as to earn a living, that year he began what was to be his last work, a film made with the Cinerama process, which, according to Frances Flaherty, "stood for everything against which he had fought all his movie life" (Rotha, ed. Ruby 271). In April, Flaherty developed pneumonia while using the new process to shoot the Chicago parade celebrating General MacArthur's return from Korea. His health failed rapidly, and on 23 July 1951, at the age of sixty-seven, Robert Flaherty died in New York City of a cerebral thrombosis. He is buried on his farm in Black Mountain, Vermont.

CHAPTER NINE

The Artist as Visionary

I

Popular society has firmly established notions of what it means to be an artist in America. An artist is either an individual at odds with the conventional world, free from customs, or a dweller in some special land hardly aware of the world and its practical demands. Those who hold these views generally agree that art is concerned with permanent values, not transient ones, and that its ultimate statement is general, not specific. What we call social consciousness, the artist's awareness of a personal responsibility for the general good, is a relatively new idea in the history of art. In the history of cinema, however, the role of the artist as analyst of society has tended to prevail over that of the artist as alienated rebel, and has inspired some outstanding nonfiction films, notably those of the Soviet school of silent montage and those of the British school of documentary that was influenced by Sergei Eisenstein, Dziga Vertov, Joris Ivens, and others active in European filmmaking of the late 1920s and 1930s.

Robert Flaherty's career is unusual in nonfiction film, in that it seems to typify the popular tripartite view of the artist: rebel, bohemian, and visionary. Rebelling against the conventional, he lived the nomadic life of a man committed to his art, going his own way and seeing life as he wanted it to be. His humanistic values often put him at odds with a film industry where profits came first. Although he tried all his life to control the production of his films, his history as an artist is one of compromises and feuds. Thus, it is not surprising that his highly personal, selective way of photographing life and his contentious relationships with his colleagues resulted, more often than not, in films that only partially examined what he set out to explore. Moreover, while he was aware of the realities of the modern world around him, with the exception of *The Land,* there is seldom evident in his work any of the social consciousness we associate with the documentary film. Flaherty was a conservative, and his two attempts at making a Griersonian

Flaherty, shortly before his death, in New York's Chelsea
Hotel.

documentary—*Industrial Britain* and *The Land*—did not altogether fulfill
Grierson's liberal aspirations for the realist documentary film *(Grierson on
Documentary* 151).

Flaherty's view of the world was founded not only on a humanistic faith
in man but also on a romantic neglect of human evil. This tender vision

embraces the human, not the material continuum of this world. Flaherty agreed with Rousseau that the most primitive and the least advanced peoples are the happiest and the least corrupt, and like Rousseau, Flaherty believed that the arts and sciences that comprise what we call civilization actually corrupt man's native goodness. But, unlike Rousseau, who never traveled to distant countries, Flaherty confirmed his belief through world travels. In fact, his travels served as a means of escape, for he succeeded in ignoring the unpleasant aspects of life—human exploitation, corruption, and misery—that he found everywhere he went to make films. His passionate love of life—of people, animals, the earth itself—seems to have been all he needed in the way of preparation for exploring whatever geography, temporal or spatial, that intrigued him. He sought places—all of them corrupted by the time he reached them—where there were sufficient basic materials to permit him to fulfill this romantic vision as well as to create films that would give pleasure to his audiences.[158] Believing in mankind's essential goodness, he did not depict man's oppression of man. His films are travelogues to places that never were; they charm (but do not instruct) audiences with their narrative simplicity and cinematographic beauty.

We cannot simply identify Flaherty either as a "documentary" filmmaker—one whose commentary and criticism should address issues of social inequity or injustice—or as a realist filmmaker—one who uses cinematic technique to re-present reality. He was a pioneer in exploration and in filmmaking, and the technical shortcomings in his approach seem a necessary part of his searching for and discovering the potential of his art. A mystic in the modern age, Flaherty was a lovable and loving man whose films (if not his life) suggest that he was somewhat out of touch with an age torn by world wars, social and economic upheaval, and shifting moral values. In response to this fragmented world, he created a myth that combined the imaginary and the real—the noble savage, the seasons of the year, and the rhythms of life—a myth that gained its lasting validity from the strength of Flaherty's conception. He believed equally in his two creations: his mythical world and his mythical self.

II

Even though Flaherty habitually transforms reality in ways that defy classification by the traditional nonfiction genres—factual, documentary, ethnographic—his essential achievement is that of the realist filmmaker. Realism, the broadest term in art, can be defined as that element in film concerned with giving a truthful impression of actuality as it appears to the normal human consciousness. Flaherty's subjective view of reality—his "making it all up"—has a romantic basis, idealizing the simple, natural, and even nonexistent life, but it also achieves a realistic image through location shooting, straight cinematography, and fidelity in editing to temporal and spatial actuality.

Generally, the realist filmmaker who modifies natural appearances stops short of the point where modification becomes distortion. However, the world as Flaherty found it did not often agree with the world as he imagined and wanted it to be, so he invented narrative and characters ("told lies," as Plato has it) or took liberties with facts (as in *Man of Aran* when he sent people out to hunt sharks years after such pursuits had ended or in *Louisiana Story* when he staged the fight between the boy and the alligator). While this achieved some effects that might otherwise have been unattainable, it was not faithful to actuality and did not offer a model that *re*presents reality. Still, however much Flaherty may have distorted reality, it was not with the deceptive, propagandistic intentions of a film such as Leni Riefenstahl's *Triumph of the Will* (1935).[159] We need only contrast Flaherty's approach to life with, say, Luis Buñuel's in *Las Hurdes (Land without Bread,* 1932) to conclude that, despite their fictional elements, Flaherty's films are more realistic than not. According to a prefatory title, Buñuel's film is a "study of human geography." Flaherty's essays in human geography—that is to say, people in their environment—are straightforward, as far away from a film like Buñuel's as naturalism is from surrealism. Buñuel reveals his people through cruelty (the word is André Bazin's), Flaherty through love (the word is Jean Renoir's). Buñuel's surrealistic approach permits him to see through to what Bazin calls "the bottom of reality," while Flaherty's realism explores the surfaces for their narrative potential.[160] Ultimately, both filmmakers affirm human dignity.

Two formal aspects of his work place Flaherty firmly within the theoretical configuration of the realist tradition: his dependence on cinematography, rather than editing, and his reliance on long-focus lenses. Flaherty's use of the long take, of re-framing to follow what is of interest, and of depth-of-field cinematography preserves the unities of place and action and creates a potentially rich ambiguity of meaning. As a cinematographer, he had an intuitive (some say "innocent") eye for capturing temporal and spatial reality. His perspectives imply a single, fixed viewpoint that remains stable even as the natural world is in flux. Realistic also are the human truth and natural beauty in his films, even though they derive from his humanism and skill as a cinematographer rather than from his fidelity to truth.

A realistic "look," however, does not necessarily make a realist film. Until the last decade of his career, the primary obstacles to Flaherty's pursuit of cinematic realism were his disregard of editing and sound. Working with the Inuit Eskimos in making *Nanook,* Flaherty learned the basic organic principle that style should emerge from within the subject matter, through the selection and arrangement of details. But, in his case, practice differed from theory. He shot hundreds of thousands of feet of film, responding not only to the dictates of his "found story," but also to the requirements of his preconceptions. This method results in an extraordinary ratio of footage shot to that which is incorporated in the final cut. The advantage of not using a shooting script, a technique that many years later became central to direct cinema,[161] is that it permits the filmmaker to explore the subject freely and to realize his own vision. But this technique seldom produces impressive results without the masterful editing evidenced in the work of such "direct cinema" advocates as Frederick Wiseman or Albert and David Maysles.[162] All too often, the process becomes chaotic for the editor, especially if that editor is not also the photographer. Flaherty had little interest in either the theory or practice of editing until editor Helen Van Dongen joined him on *The Land* in 1940 for the first of their two collaborations. As for sound, although he experimented earlier with narration and music, it was not until his last film, *Louisiana Story,* that he took seriously the direct, realistic recording of sound. Whatever the indisputable strengths of the early films, Flaherty's unwillingess to plan ahead, his reliance on assembling rather than editing his footage, and his reluctance to use sound more realistically have earned for these early films a controversial place in the overall development of nonfiction film realism.

III

The only point on which most theorists of realist film agree is, according to Christopher Williams, that it "should in some sense be truthful or tell the truth" (79). Van Dongen, Grierson, Kracauer, and Bazin—in their writing about Flaherty—all address this question of truth. Williams observes: "We have to balance Kracauer's belief that Flaherty is not interested in stories, and particularly not in individual stories, with the contrary assertion from Grierson and the clear evidence from Van Dongen that the beginning of *Louisiana Story* is constructed, precisely, as the beginning of a story" (103). V. F. Perkins offers another perspective from which to study Flaherty's realism: "On one level cinematic credibility is no different from that which we demand of other story-telling forms. It depends on the inner consistency of the created world" (quoted in Williams 69). Flaherty understood that this elastic conception of cinematographic realism provided him with new areas to explore and with opportunities to develop a narrative style that imposed fictional form on fact and combined interpretation with documentation. In creating his cinematic world, Flaherty may not always have made films that were true to the facts, but they are true to his vision.

In his study of existence in relation to itself and not in relation to himself, Flaherty's work is often associated with anthropology. Like many anthropologists, he was fascinated by a way of life that was long since gone; however, in contrast to orthodox anthropological practice, in *Nanook of the North, Moana,* and *Man of Aran,* he turned back the clock, altering such things as the way his subjects lived, dressed, and hunted, and paying them for playing this charade with him. This approach, harmless as it may seem, suggests an indifference to deeper social, psychological, and economic realities. The process of filming can have unforeseen effects on those being filmed, as Claude Lévi-Strauss found in studying Brazilian natives; not only did the Brazilians insist on being paid before they would pose for pictures, but, the bargain made, they actually forced him to photograph them in order to get their wages (156). Flaherty paid Nanook and the other Inuit people for their work, as he was to do throughout his career with others who appeared in his films, knowing, as Barnouw observed, that this approach would alter the people and events being filmed and re-create the past through two viewpoints: his own and the natives' *(Documentary* 36). Fascinated with the simple rituals of the Inuit, the Samoan, and the Aran Islander, Flaherty could overlook the complex human needs, human interrelationships, and ecological relationships that characterize any people or culture, including those that are called "primitive."[163]

Flaherty sought, by means of his camera, to create images that would somehow restore the older way of life. Thus, he reached the Canadian sub-Arctic and learned that the Inuit people had encountered the white man some 100 years before he reached their hunting grounds, that their clothes, tools, methods of hunting, means of shelter—in short, everything that formed their previous culture—had been changed, if not destroyed. Before beginning *Nanook of the North,* Flaherty and Nanook agreed that the process of filming reality would take precedence over the life being filmed. Confronted with charges that he restaged scenes, Flaherty said: "Sometimes you have to lie. One often has to distort a thing to catch its true spirit" (quoted in Calder-Marshall 97). Then, as now, his audiences probably did not know that changes had taken place; since this was a remote region to which very few white men had traveled, or would ever travel, they were satisfied with images that corroborated what they believed to be true.

Similarly, Flaherty breaks rank with the anthropologists and ethnographers in his assumption that the truth is to be found not in the past revealed by the methods and tools of scientific inquiry but in the past imagined and re-created for his camera.[164] This process is found also in history painting, another narrative genre, in which factual reality is replaced by fictional creation that subsequent generations may either accept or challenge with new evidence. In film, the viewer's principles and tastes ultimately decide whether or not the filmmaker's vision and images are valid.[165] Flaherty's humanistic vision is valid because of the vigor with which he believed in it and the dedication with which he created cinematic images to express it.

Today, we may attempt to calculate the margin by which Flaherty missed his opportunities to preserve what would have been imperishable docu-ments of real life, as it was lived at the moment in which Flaherty pho-tographed it, not imagined life, as it was lived at a time before Flaherty. His romanticism, desire to tell stories, and control as an *auteur* all precluded the control and validation of the scientific method. Instead, Flaherty relied on his knowledge about the past, his intuition about the present, and his freedom to explore and improvise as he went along. Moreover, he knew that audiences did not always expect a faithful representation of reality, that they preferred the relatively superior craft of fiction films, and that nonfic-tion films attracted them with such devices as restaging. Kevin Brownlow writes:

> The bizarre truth is that the most effective films of fact have been subject to almost as much manipulation as fiction films. The more astounding they look, the less authentic they are.
>
> The gulf between the so-called pure documentary, which records only actuality, and the reconstructed documentary, which is branded a fake, is not as broad as we have been led to suppose. There are precious few documen-taries that have *not* resorted to some kind of restaging. Robert Flaherty, regarded as the purest film-maker of all, had no compunction about present-ing his own romantic vision rather than unadulterated reality. (409)

This is particularly true of Flaherty's early audiences, when cinema was primarily an entertaining novelty.

In theory, Robert Flaherty believed that the real world had a significance that would be revealed only if he did not impose on it his own ideas of that significance. However, in making most of his films, he replicated a pattern, using similar motifs to tell similar stories about dissimilar people in dissimi-lar places, providing for the audience a point from which to view worlds unknown and confirming a universality of existence and spirit.[166] Flaherty realized that filmmaking is not a function of anthropology or even archeol-

Robert and Frances Flaherty on their farm in Black Mountain,
Vermont.

ogy, but an act of the imagination; it is both photographic truth and a cinematic re-arrangement of the truth. Flaherty was an artist, and thus as free as a novelist or painter to record incidents as they occurred and to use his imagination to create events.

IV

While Robert Flaherty remains today somewhat elusive, a mystery enveloped in a myth that he helped to create, his legacy is clear and unique. His films have had a lasting effect on his audiences and a lasting influence on his colleagues. Flaherty loved the natural and human world, and his films not only confirmed this love for both audiences and filmmakers, but also introduced them to new ways of seeing. He encouraged us to look at the world, not to imitate his way of seeing. There were achievements and failures in his career, but he inspired filmmakers with his realization of the dramatic potential of actual material, his resolute independence, his pursuit of his vision of life, his experimentation, his refusal to compromise, and his affirmation of the importance of narrative to filmmaking. He was an artist, and through his telling of stories, his questioning of cinematic form, and his variations on cinematic realism, he demonstrated his understanding that the ultimate picture of reality is unattainable.

1. Although Calder-Marshall's was the biography authorized by Frances Flaherty, Paul Rotha's earlier biography has recently been edited and re-issued: *Robert J. Flaherty: A Biography,* ed. Jay Ruby (Philadelphia: University of Pennsylvania Press, 1983); see Ruby's introduction (1–4) for an explanation of the relationship between the two biographies. Rotha's is the more reliable of the two, but Winston holds an extreme and opposite view: "We are here in the presence of the blarney, extensive, sustained, and assiduously cultivated blarney, initially stemming from Flaherty himself and subsequently maintained by his family and friends" (58). A good biographical summary of Flaherty's career with some new information is in William T. Murphy, *Robert Flaherty: A Guide to References and Resources* (Boston: Hall, 1978); see also Richard Meran Barsam, *Nonfiction Film: A Critical History* (New York: Dutton, 1973), Chap. 6; and "Robert Flaherty Talking," *The Cinema 1950,* ed. Roger Manvell (London: Penguin, 1950), 11–29.

2. Quoted in Calder-Marshall 72. In Rotha, ed. Ruby, this remark is quoted: "I was an explorer first and a filmmaker a long way after" (7).

3. See the following chapter for an account of the trips and filmmaking attempts preceding *Nanook of the North.*

4. For a much harsher analysis of his methods, see Winston.

5. *Looking at Photographs* (New York: Museum of Modern Art, 1973), 22.

6. John Goldman, the editor of *Man of Aran,* provides some useful observations on Flaherty's cinematographic practices in "Notes by John Goldman," in Rotha, ed. Ruby 327–30; see also interview with Richard Leacock in Levin, 210–12.

7. Flaherty quoted in Hugh Gray, "Father of the American Documentary," in *The American Cinema,* ed. Donald E. Staples (Washington: USIA, 1973), 199; quoted differently in Rotha, ed. Ruby, 5.

8. "Flaherty's *Louisiana Story,*" *The Documentary Tradition: From Nanook to Woodstock,* ed. Lewis Jacobs (New York: Hopkinson, 1971), 231; see also Ernest Callenbach, "The Understood Antagonist and Other Observations," *Film Quarterly,* 12, No. 4 (Summer 1959), 16–23.

9. For an excellent discussion of Bazin's appreciation for Flaherty, see Dudley Andrew, *André Bazin* (New York: Oxford University Press, 1978), esp. 107–12, 180–81.

10. Biographical sources for this period are Calder-Marshall, 15–26, and Rotha, ed. Ruby, 7ff.

11. Detailed accounts of his several expeditions can be found in Flaherty's writings, chiefly *My Eskimo Friends* (1924), his articles in *Geographical Review* (1918 and 1919), and his diaries, housed in the Robert Flaherty Papers in Butler Library of Columbia University, New York; see also his 1949 BBC broadcasts, relevant excerpts from which are quoted in Rotha, ed. Ruby, 12–15.

12. Flaherty, "Two Traverses across Ungava Peninsula, Labrador," *Geographical Review,* 6, No. 2, 116–32. For an account of Flaherty's connection with seventeenth-century explorers who first traveled this region, see Terry Ramsaye, "Flaherty, Great Adventurer," in George Pratt, *Spellbound in Darkness: A History of the Silent Film* (New York: New York Graphic Society, 1973), 342–54. Flaherty wrote two novels

based on these experiences: *The Captain's Chair: A Story of the North* (New York: Scribner's, 1938) and *White Master* (London: Routledge, 1939).

13. For accounts of Flaherty's still photography, see Jo-Anne Birnie Danzker, "Robert Flaherty/Photographer," *Studies in Visual Communication*, 6, No. 2 (Summer 1980), 5–32 and *Robert Flaherty: Photographer/Filmmaker, the Inuit, 1910–1922*, ed. Jo-Anne Birnie Danzker (Vancouver: Vancouver Art Gallery, 1980), 24–51.

14. In the context of cinema history, D. W. Griffith had been making films since 1908 and would release *The Birth of a Nation* within a year and a half after Flaherty's departure.

15. For Flaherty's own accounts of his trips and discoveries, see "The Belcher Islands of Hudson Bay: Their Discovery and Exploration," *Geographical Review*, 5, No. 6, 433–58; "Wetalltook's Islands," *The World's Work* (Feb. 1923), 422–33; "Winter on Wetalltook's Islands," *The World's Work* (Mar. 1923), 538–53; and *My Eskimo Friends* (Garden City: Doubleday, 1924).

16. The identity of the person(s) at Harvard is not known.

17. There is some disagreement over whether or not making a duplicate negative would have been possible. Rotha (ed. Ruby) says that it was impossible (26), but Kevin Brownlow, an expert on early film history, says successful duplicate negatives were made as early as 1904; see *The War, the West, and the Wilderness* (New York: Knopf, 1979), 475.

18. Flaherty quoted in Calder-Marshall, 77; for a slightly different version of this remark, see Rotha, ed. Ruby, 27.

19. For excerpts from Frances Flaherty's diary concerning their efforts to find supporters for a new film project, see Jay Ruby, "The Aggie Will Come First: The Demystification of Robert Flaherty," in *Robert Flaherty: Photographer/Filmmaker, the Inuit, 1910–1922*, ed. Jo-Anne Birnie Danzker (Vancouver: Vancouver Art Gallery, 1980), 69–70.

20. Flaherty agreed to Revillon's simple request that the opening titles of the film carry the phrase "Revillon Frères Presents."

21. Erik Barnouw, *Documentary: A History of the Non-Fiction Film* (New York: Oxford University Press, 1974), 36, says $35,000 was the budget, but Paul Rotha and Basil Wright, "Nanook and the North," 42, say $53,000, the same figure that Flaherty himself cites in Erik Barnouw, "Robert Flaherty (Barnouw's File)," *Film Culture*, Nos. 53–55 (Spring 1972), 164.

22. Flaherty, *My Eskimo Friends*, 126; see also Rotha, ed. Ruby, 32ff.

23. Edmund Carpenter, *Eskimo* (Toronto: University of Toronto Press, 1959).

24. Pictures and titles taken from the film are reproduced in *Nanook of the North*, ed. Robert Kraus (New York: Windmill, 1971).

25. For an account of how the igloo was actually built, see William T. Murphy, *Robert Flaherty: A Guide to References and Resources*, 8.

26. In his analysis of Chaplin's *The Gold Rush* (1925), Gerald Mast suggests that Flaherty might have influenced Chaplin's view of life in the frozen wastes; see *A Short History of the Movies*, 3rd ed. (Indianapolis: Bobbs-Merrill, 1981), 124.

27. Quoted in Calder-Marshall, *The Innocent Eye: The Life of Robert J. Flaherty*, 97. As Jean Renoir noted, this method of engaging our curiosity makes it seem that Flaherty made the picture for each individual member of the audience (Calder-Marshall, 95).

28. For a different view, see Ruby, "The Aggie Will Come First," 67–68.

29. Flaherty's task was to document how Nanook survived, not to help him survive. Nanook's death, two years after the film was released, was not due to any neglect on Flaherty's part.

30. Bazin, *What Is Cinema?*, I (Berkeley: University of California Press, 1967), 27;

154–63. For an analysis of a scene from *Nanook* that demonstrates how much Flaherty yields from moving the camera and thus re-framing to continue coverage of a single action, see Laurence Goldstein and Jay Kaufman, *Into Film* (New York: Dutton, 1976), 27–28.

31. Flaherty assembled the footage in *Nanook* with the assistance of Charles Gelb, a technician otherwise inexperienced with film editing.

32. These problems do not include the uneven photographic quality of the images, which is due in large measure to the erratic climatic conditions in which the film was made, not to any failure on his part to control it.

33. There was, however, a "music plot" provided to original exhibitors; see "The Campaign Book for Exhibitors," *Studies in Visual Communication*, 6, No. 2 (Summer 1980), 74. For accounts of authenticating and restoring *Nanook*, see David Shepard, "Authenticating Films," *The Quarterly Journal of the Library of Congress*, 37, Nos. 3–4 (Summer-Fall 1980), 342–54; and Steve Dobi, "Restoring Robert Flaherty's *Nanook of the North*," *Film Library Quarterly*, 10, Nos. 1–2 (1977), 6–18.

34. Both films were reviewed favorably in the *New York Times* (12 June 1922), 10:2. Flaherty recalled that *Nanook* was booked on a double bill with *Grandma's Boy*, Harold Lloyd's first feature film, but his brother David contradicted this and said it opened as the sole feature and ran a week (Rotha, ed. Ruby, 43–44). However, the *New York Times* appears to be correct in saying that *Nanook* and *My Country* opened together and were both held over for two weeks. *Grandma's Boy* opened on 4 September 1922 at the Strand Theater in New York City; see the *New York Times* (4 Sept. 1922), 14:4.

35. "The Campaign Book for Exhibitors," 61–76.

36. Barnouw, *Documentary: A History of the Non-Fiction Film*, 43; it also inspired a string quartet, "Night," by Swiss born composer Ernest Bloch.

37. For a summary of *Nanook*'s critical reception, see William T. Murphy, *Robert Flaherty: A Guide to References and Resources*, 55–62; see also Paul Rotha and Basil Wright, "Nanook of the North," *Studies in Visual Communication*, 6, No. 2 (Summer 1980), 49–58.

38. Iris Barry, *Let's Go to the Pictures* (London: Chatto, 1926), 57. See also Vilhjalmur Stafansson, *The Standardization of Error* (London: Kegan, 1929). For a summary of charges against the film, see William T. Murphy, *Robert Flaherty: A Guide to References and Resources*, 57.

39. Thus, Paramount, under Lasky, became the first and thereafter almost the only American studio to support large nonfiction film production in the late 1920s. For a summary of Lasky's interests, see Rotha, ed. Ruby, 52ff. Shortly after signing Flaherty, Lasky signed Merian C. Cooper and Ernst B. Schoedsack to make *Grass* (1925).

40. For historical and biographical background, see Rotha, ed. Ruby, Chap. 2 and Calder-Marshall, Chaps. 8, 9, and 10.

41. Among these friends was Frederick O'Brien, whose *White Shadows of the South Seas* (New York: Century, 1919) ironically turned out to cast some of the darkest shadows on Flaherty's career from 1923 until the experience with *Tabu: A Story of the South Seas* was over in 1929.

42. The titles for *Moana* in prints circulated by the Museum of Modern Art do not include a credit for director. Instead, the main title reads: "Moana / A Romance of the Golden Age / by Robert J. Flaherty, F.R.G.S. / (Producer [sic] of 'Nanook of the North') / and Frances Hubbard Flaherty." The second title reads: "Produced by Robert J. and Frances Hubbard Flaherty." For an account of a film about Frances Flaherty, see Peter Werner, "Frances Flaherty: Hidden and Seeking," *Film Makers' Newsletter*, Nos. 9–10 (July-Aug. 1972), 28–30. See also Calder-Marshall, 99.

43. For a summary of the production history of *Moana,* see Rotha, ed. Ruby, 54–73.

44. See Calder-Marshall, 109–11; Murphy, 14; and Robert Flaherty, "Picture Making in the South Seas," *Film Daily Yearbook—1924,* 9–13, and "The Most Unforgettable Character I've Met," *Reader's Digest,* 40, No. 239 (March 1942), 41–44.

45. *Argonauts of the Western Pacific* (New York: Dutton, 1922), 25. I am grateful to George F. Custen for suggesting this parallel between Flaherty's work and that of other early ethnographers.

46. Since Moana is being covered with patterns from the waist to the knees, it seems valid to inquire if the genitals were also tattooed. The sexually explicit nature of the dance that precedes and follows the tattooing, as well as the presence of fiancée and family, also points toward genital mutilation through tattooing.

47. Dziga Vertov observed that "the film drama is the opium of the people"; quoted in *Realism and the Cinema,* ed. Christopher Williams (London: Routledge, 1980), 25.

48. William T. Murphy (15) writes:

> The Flahertys had seen two persons tattooed previously. Although tattooing was officially discouraged, others have said that the practice was widespread. The Flaherty's believed it was one of those aspects of Samoan culture that was going to disappear, and so they would capture it on film.

49. Still unresolved is Frances Flaherty's exact contribution to Robert Flaherty's career. For an insight into their relationship, see Calder-Marshall, 244–51; see also Leo Dratfield, "Robert Flaherty's Daughter Remembers: An Interview with Frances Flaherty Rohr," *Sightlines* (Fall/Winter 1984/85), 11–14.

50. *The Odyssey of a Film-Maker,* 20; see also Frances Flaherty, "Explorations," in *Film Book I: The Audience and the Filmmaker,* ed. Robert Hughes (New York: Grove, 1959), 61–65.

51. "Setting Up House and Shop in Samoa," *Asia* (Aug. 1925), 639–51ff; "Behind the Scenes with our Samoan Stars," *Asia* (Sept. 1925), 747–53ff; "A Search for Animal [sic] and Sea Sequence," *Asia* (Nov. 1925), 954–62ff; "Fa'A-Samoa," *Asia* (Dec. 1925), 1085–90ff; "The Camera's Eye," and a work based largely on these articles: *Samoa* (Berlin: Hobbing, 1932). See also David Flaherty, "Serpents in Eden," *Asia* (Oct. 1925), 858–69ff.

52. Brownlow, 482. See Calder-Marshall, 108–109, for the source of some of the confusion over Flaherty's use of panchromatic stock, which is repeated in my *Nonfiction Film: A Critical History,* 136, as well as in Murphy, 13–14 and in Rotha, ed. Ruby, 62ff.

53. *What Is Cinema?,* I, (Berkeley: University of California Press, 1967), 162; today's viewer must secure a perfect print to see this virtue in *Moana.*

54. For Richard Leacock's comments on Flaherty's cinematography, see G. Roy Levin, *Documentary Explorations: Fifteen Interviews with Film-Makers* (Garden City: Doubleday, 1971), 210–12.

55. It was David Flaherty who said that Robert and Frances Flaherty did the work; see Rotha, ed. Ruby, 71.

56. Grierson quoted in Elizabeth Sussex, *The Rise and Fall of British Documentary: The Story of the Film Movement Founded by John Grierson* (Berkeley: University of California Press, 1975), 3. See the entire passage for further background on how Grierson came to use the word; see also John Grierson, *Grierson on Documentary,* ed. Forsyth Hardy (London: Faber, 1966), 145.

57. The recent release of *Moana* with a musical soundtrack is the work of Flaherty's daughter Monica and Richard Leacock; see Leacock, "*Moana* with Music," *Sight and Sound* 54, No. 1 (Winter 1984–85), 4–5.

58. For historical and biographical background, see Calder-Marshall, Chaps. 10, 11; and Rotha, ed. Ruby, Chaps. 2, 3.

59. While Robert Flaherty was making the first two of these films, he was forced to break the family pattern and was apart from Frances Flaherty and their children, and there is no evidence that his wife worked with him in any significant way on either of them. However, in June 1929, when working with Murnau, he wrote that "I loathe this contriving—this story business—when we can, you and I, do such memorable things. When all these things are over, Moana will shine as it has always shone." Letter quoted in Mark J. Langer, "*Tabu:* The Making of a Film," *Cinema Journal* 24.3 (Spring 1985), 51.

60. See Donald H. Clarke, "Producer of *Nanook* Joins Metro-Goldwyn," in George C. Pratt, *Spellbound in Darkness,* 347–48; and Lewis Jacobs, *The Rise of the American Film* (New York: Columbia University Teachers College Press, 1968), 543–82.

61. Brownlow, 484, writes that *Twenty-Four Dollar Island* was "shown with a [Mauritz] Stiller picture at the Fifth Avenue Playhouse, and eventually used as a backdrop for a stage ballet at the Roxy Theater. This was not the insult it has been made out to be. S. L. Rothapfel (Roxy) genuinely admired the film and surrounded it with an exclusive presentation." Regarding this theatrical use of the film, I am grateful to Brownlow for correcting my error in *Nonfiction Film: A Critical History,* 141.

62. Rare examples of successful films made through a collaboration of directors include the early adventure films and thrillers made by Ernest B. Schoedsack and Merian C. Cooper (*Grass,* 1926; *Chang,* 1927; *The Four Feathers,* 1929; and *King Kong,* 1933, among others), and the Hollywood musicals directed by Gene Kelly and Stanley Donen or Vincente Minnelli (*The Pirate,* 1948; *On the Town,* 1949; *An American in Paris,* 1951; and *Singin' in the Rain,* 1952).

63. Langer, 46; neither Calder-Marshall, Rotha, nor Murphy mention this brief collaboration with McCarthy.

64. Flaherty's actual credit on the film depends on the print. His name does not appear in the credits of some of the rental prints currently available, but he is given credit for "Additional Directing" in *The American Film Institute Catalog of Motion Pictures Produced in the United States: Feature Films 1921–1930,* II, ed. Kenneth Munden (New York and London: Bowker, 1971), 895. Richard Griffith (*The World of Robert Flaherty,* Duell, 1953, 76) estimates that Flaherty contributed to a scant dozen shots in the film. Rotha (ed. Ruby, 85, reports an M-G-M contemporary's account that Flaherty made contributions to the screenplay and to the casting.

65. See Brownlow, 485–90, for an account of Murnau's work on this project. During this period, Murnau also made "Our Daily Bread," released as *City Girl* (1931).

66. Flaherty had earlier hoped to make a picture on the island of Bali in the Dutch East Indies, first alone and then later with Murnau, but nothing came of the project; see Barnouw, "Robert Flaherty (Barnouw's File)," 161–85.

67. For a thorough account of the problems they encountered, see Langer; for another version of their differences, see Richard Griffith, "Flaherty and *Tabu,*" *Film Culture,* 20 (1959), 12–13.

68. Correspondence from Murnau to Flaherty and from Flaherty to Frances Flaherty in collection of catalogued correspondence in the Flaherty Papers, Columbia University, New York.

69. In preparing the final print, Murnau also tried to deny Floyd Crosby the screen credit he deserved; Crosby, whose credit finally appeared as it should have, won an Academy Award for the cinematography; see Langer, 57–58.

70. For the original outline and script in story form, see Robert Flaherty, "Tabu, A Story of the South Seas" and "Turia, An Original Story," *Film Culture,* 20 (1959), 17–38.

71. Flaherty quoted in Hugh Gray, "Father of the American Documentary," in *The American Cinema,* ed. Donald E. Staples (Washington: USIA, 1973), 199; quoted differently in Rotha, ed. Ruby, 5. Glass-bottomed excursion boats were popular with tourists who wanted to see the underwater life at Catalina Island, off the Southern California coast.

72. For a history of the British documentary film movement, see Barsam, *Nonfiction Film: A Critical History,* 37–80; Sussex; Paul Rotha, *Documentary Diary: An Informal History of the British Documentary Film, 1928–1939* (New York: Hill, 1973); Forsyth Hardy, *John Grierson: A Documentary Biography* (London: Faber, 1979).

73. Rotha, *Documentary Diary,* 50; Sussex, 23–43.

74. Flaherty quoted in Calder-Marshall, 137. However, a preliminary scenario, titled "Craftsmanship" [sic], signed by Robert Flaherty, dated 27 August 1931, is in Box 28, Flaherty Papers, Columbia University, New York. Although it does not altogether resemble the completed film, it shows careful thought and feeling for the subject.

75. See Hardy, *John Grierson,* 65ff; for a slightly different version, see Elizabeth Sussex, 26.

76. For other production background of *Industrial Britain,* see Rotha, ed. Ruby, 95–106; Calder-Marshall, 130–40; and Murphy, 20–22.

77. Stories of Flaherty's extravagance are a large part of his legend; for a good example, see Harry Watt's comments in Sussex, 31.

78. About *The English Potter,* one of the films made from this material, Grierson said: "It was one of the most beautiful films I ever saw in my life. . . . It was the quintessence of Flaherty, because there's nothing to beat Flaherty behind a camera" (Grierson quoted in Sussex, 25). For a perceptive account of Flaherty's use of cinematography, lighting, and camera movement, see Edgar Anstey, "Development of Film Technique in Britain," in *Experiment in the Film,* ed. Roger Manvell (New York: Arno, 1970), 245–46.

79. *John Grierson,* 65. This package consisted of *Industrial Britain, The Country Comes to Town, O'er Hill and Dale, Upstream, The Shadow on the Mountain,* and *King Log.*

80. William Troy, "Film: Pure Cinema," *The Nation,* 139, No. 3617 (Oct. 31, 1934), 518; see also Troy, "Films: Behind the Scenes," *The Nation,* 141, No. 3563 (July 10, 1935), 56.

81. For biographical and historical background, see Calder-Marshall, Chaps. 12, 13; Rotha, ed. Ruby, Chap. 3.

82. Calder-Marshall, 142. See also Grierson, *Grierson on Documentary,* 176; Michael Balcon et al., *Twenty Years of British Film: 1925–1947* (London: Falcon, 1947).

83. For a different version of Flaherty's first acquaintance with Synge's work, see Murphy, 22. For biographical, personal, and production information on the making of the film, see these articles by Robert Flaherty: "Account of Making the Film—*Man of Aran,*" Box 31, Flaherty Papers, Columbia University; "Filming Real People," in *The Documentary Tradition: From Nanook to Woodstock,* ed. Lewis Jacobs (New York: Hopkinson, 1971), 97–99; "Robert Flaherty Tells How He Made *Man of Aran,*" *National Board of Review Magazine,* 10, No. 1 (Jan. 1935), 5–7. See also

Frances Flaherty, *The Odyssey of a Film-Maker,* 24–33; Murphy, 22–28; and Calder-Marshall, 141–72.

84. J. M. Synge, *The Aran Islands* (Boston: Luce, 1911), 20. See also Synge, *Riders to the Sea,* in *A Treasury of the Theatre,* ed. John Gassner (New York: Simon, 1960), 628–732.

85. For a colorful, detailed account of Flaherty's travels with his two collaborators—Frances Flaherty and John Goldman—and the making of the film, see Pat Mullen, *Man of Aran* (Cambridge: MIT Press, 1970). In 1978, George Stoney released *How the Myth Was Made,* a color film dealing with the making of *Man of Aran.*

86. Their lightweight boat is known as a *curragh.*

87. While Flaherty had used the wind as a character in *Nanook,* this bolder conception of nature as a character recalls Victor Sjostrom's *The Wind* (1928), where the wind, representing a cold and loveless world, drives a woman (played by Lillian Gish) mad.

88. André Bazin stated that this fidelity to fact is "one of the consequences of photographic realism." *What Is Cinema?,* I, 102–103.

89. This use of music illustrates Siegfried Kracauer's point that "to sustain a visual theme and to overemphasize it is [sic] two different things. Parallel commentative music may be so outspoken or obtrusive that it no longer functions as an accompaniment but assumes a leading position." See Kracauer, *Theory of Film: The Redemption of Physical Reality* (New York: Oxford University Press, 1960), 141.

90. In actual fact, Tiger-King is not even in the boat; the work was so dangerous that only the experts were permitted to go out in the storm. See Gray, "Father of the American Documentary," 208.

91. For a different view of Flaherty's distortions of actuality, see Hugh Gray, "Robert Flaherty and the Naturalistic Documentary," *Hollywood Quarterly,* 5, No. 1 (Fall 1950), 41–48.

92. By contrast, Georges Rouquier's *Farrebique* (1946), a film influenced by Flaherty, presents actuality without a staged conflict and structures the cinematic time to reflect the natural cycles of change throughout one year.

93. Robert Flaherty, "Filming Real People," 99. John Taylor was second cameraman; see interview with Taylor in Sussex, 28.

94. For an account of Flaherty's work with the cast and shooting the storm sequence, see Frances Flaherty, "How *Man of Aran* Came into Being," *Film News,* 13, No. 3 (1953), 4–6. See also Mullen, 188–99.

95. See Calder-Marshall, 157–63; see also Hugh Gray, "Father of the American Documentary," 204–205.

96. See "Notes by John Goldman" in Rotha, ed. Ruby, 327–30.

97. In 1927, Frances Flaherty praised Eisenstein's *Potemkin,* saying "there has recently been exhibited a Russian film that uses the camera in this way. An historical incident has been re-enacted, and then, over these re-enacted scenes the camera has been brought to play as over actual life, and the result is that same conviction of reality. This Russian film and the two films we have made *[Nanook* and *Moana]* must be thought of as experiments. The principle is there. Its development will come." See Mrs. Robert J. Flaherty, "The Camera's Eye," in George C. Pratt, *Spellbound in Darkness: A History of the Silent Film* (New York: New York Graphic Society, 1973), 347. With typical exaggeration, Flaherty himself said that more than anything else he was influenced by the Russian cinema of the 1920s. See Penelope Houston, "Interview with Flaherty," *Sight and Sound* (Jan. 1950), 16.

98. During the filming, Flaherty was very much concerned with the safety of his

cast, for his re-enactment of the shark hunt placed great responsibility on his shoulders. See Mullen, 99–118. Another treatment of a similar narrative problem can be found in Luchino Visconti's film *La Terra Trema* (1948).

99. Excited by the Russian films he had seen, Flaherty wanted to make films in the Soviet Union, but the Russians were not enthusiastic about his proposed projects.

100. A good example is "Snakes!" in Rotha, ed. Ruby, 310–11.

101. For historical and biographical background in the making of this film, see Rotha, ed. Ruby, 161–88; Calder-Marshall, 173–84; and Murphy, 29–30.

102. Alexander Korda was primarily a producer, but between 1914 and 1947, he directed 58 films: 25 in Hungary, 4 in Vienna, 6 in Berlin, 10 in Hollywood, 6 in Paris, and 7 in Great Britain.

103. Karol Kulik, *Alexander Korda: The Man Who Could Work Miracles* (New Rochelle: Arlington, 1975), 135. See also Jeffrey Richards, *Visions of Yesterday* (London: Routledge, 1973).

104. Rotha, ed. Ruby, 163–64, provides an account of their meeting over the contract, as well as two differing accounts.

105. In "Elephant Boy," *World Film News*, 1:12, 5, Grierson wrote:

> It takes Flaherty to remind us that we film people live in two worlds and the two, Kipling fashion, do not often meet. The studio mind does not understand the realist mind, nor *vice versa*. One hopes continually a producer will arise who will take a genius for great observation like Flaherty's and not combine it naturally with the orders of the studio. Korda has not in this case quite succeeded in being that producer.

106. Calder-Marshall, 183, writes that Flaherty remained on the payroll of London Films and helped in the promotion of *Elephant Boy*.

107. Osmond Borradaile, the cinematographer on *Elephant Boy*, wrote with insight about Flaherty's character and working methods; see Rotha, ed. Ruby, 173.

108. *Elephant Dance* (New York: Scribner's, 1937), 13–14. This book consists of letters written to the Flahertys' two younger daughters in school in England and provides a charming, impressionistic account of their travels. However, it says virtually nothing about making the film and gives no indication whatever that there were any problems. The problems are related in Calder-Marshall, 173–84, and Rotha, ed. Ruby, 165–77.

109. See Rotha, ed. Ruby, 185, for information on a similar project, the adaptation of "Boy and the Pit Pony," and 231 for the report that Flaherty sold the "Bonito the Bull" subject to Orson Welles for $12,000 in 1942. Welles incorporated it into *It's All True*, his controversial, unreleased fiction/nonfiction trilogy; the Flaherty story, directed by Norman Foster, was titled "My Friend Bonito"; see Barbara Leaming, *Orson Welles: A Biography* (New York: Penguin, 1986), 270ff.

110. In 1927, the American actress Maude Adams tried to raise funds so that Flaherty could make a film based on Kipling's *Kim*, but this project was never realized. Although there is no evidence that Flaherty and Kipling ever met, a minor coincidence further links them. Kipling lived in Brattleboro, Vermont, from 1892 to 1896; Flaherty moved to the nearby village of Dummerston in 1942, and on his death in 1951, he was buried there. Kipling died in 1936, the year before *Elephant Boy* was released.

111. Rotha, ed. Ruby, 178, suggests that Flaherty's emphasis on the theme of oneness with nature, so true to Indian philosophy and religion, may have been cut from the film before the final release print was made.

112. See Frances Flaherty, *Sabu: The Elephant Boy* (New York: Oxford University Press, 1937).

113. In the film, this is obviously a model sequence in which shots of elephants' feet are printed to appear to be moving forward and backward in simulation of a rhythmic dance.

114. Petersen is played by Walter Hudd, often typecast as the aloof British gentleman.

115. Rotha, ed. Ruby, 176. In *Elephant Dance,* Frances Flaherty recounts how the dangers they encountered in the Indian jungles affected their work on the film, but John Grierson comments sharply on what Korda did in London to complete the film; see "The Course of Realism," in *Grierson on Documentary,* 204.

116. The sound is weakened further by John Greenwood's musical score; Greenwood also wrote the score for *Man of Aran.*

117. Venice juries liked Flaherty's work, for they had already honored *Man of Aran* and would later honor *Louisiana Story.*

118. For a summary of the film's critical reception, see Murphy, 74–76. *Elephant Boy* is noted mainly in cinema history for its introduction of Sabu, who became a featured player in such Alexander Korda productions as *The Drum* (1938), *The Thief of Bagdad* (1940), and *Jungle Book* (1942), and later in Hollywood.

119. Throughout *Sabu,* her account of the filming of *Elephant Boy,* Mrs. Flaherty refers to her husband as the "Borah Sahib," or great white chief.

120. For an account of the origin and production problems of *The Land,* see Robert L. Snyder, *Pare Lorentz and the Documentary Film* (Norman: University of Oklahoma Press, 1968), 131–40.

121. For historical background and critical appraisal of American nonfiction filmmaking in the 1930s, see Barsam, *Nonfiction Film: A Critical History,* 81–123; Richard Dyer MacCann, *The People's Films: A Political History of U.S. Government Motion Pictures* (New York: Hastings, 1973), 43–117; and William Alexander, *Film on the Left: American Documentary Film from 1931 to 1942* (Princeton: Princeton University Press, 1981).

122. The following cable, from Lorentz to Flaherty, dated 30 May 1939, is in Box 42, Flaherty Papers, Columbia University, New York:

> Are you interested in working with Government Documentary Film Service? You would produce short saga American agriculture under Fifty Thousand Dollar budget. Unable pay more than government wage probably one seventy five weekly. Government furnishes research and scientific advice you in complete charge production would be honored having you work with me. Advise.

123. Neither Robert nor Frances Flaherty, both of whom ordinarily wrote several articles about each film, had anything to say in print about making *The Land.* Flaherty, however, was quoted in two interviews, those with Penelope Houston and Theodore Strauss cited in this chapter.

124. Mike Weaver, 18.

125. It is worthwhile to compare *The Land* with Humphrey Jennings's *Spring Offensive* (1940).

126. For a detailed, scene-by-scene reading of the film, see Mike Weaver, *Robert Flaherty's "The Land"* (Exeter, England: American Arts Documentation Centre, University of Exeter, 1979); for a synopsis that alternates passages of narration with brief descriptions of the visuals they accompany, see Rotha, ed. Ruby, 205–21.

127. John Huston is quoted in Calder-Marshall, 196, as saying that this moment was worth all of John Ford's *The Grapes of Wrath*.

128. For comments by George Gercke, a member of the crew, see Robert L. Snyder, *Pare Lorentz and the Documentary Film*, 136–37.

129. Mike Weaver, *Robert Flaherty's "The Land,"* 17–18.

130. For an account of their first meeting, see Van Dongen, in Barsam, 212–20.

131. Van Dongen, in Rotha, ed. Ruby, 200.

132. An early "trial draft" of the script is printed in Russell and Kate Lord, *Forever the Land* (New York: Harper, 1950), 29–36, the final script in Calder-Marshall, 261–79. See also Russell Lord, *Behold Our Land* (Boston: Houghton, 1938); Russell Lord, "Robert Flaherty Rediscovers America: Editorial Notes and Forthcoming Motion Picture," *The Land*, 1, No. 1 (Winter 1941), 67–75.

133. Snyder, 138. Russell Lord is quoted in Rotha, ed. Ruby, 190: "He still had the eye of an explorer when he went out to film *The Land*."

134. Richard Dyer MacCann wrote: "Essentially a silent picture, and a disconnected one at that, *The Land* is a puzzling series of shots punctuated by fade-outs, as if Flaherty expected to link them with printed titles" (100–101).

135. In Rotha, ed. Ruby, 204, Arnell recounts his only quarrel with Flaherty:

> Flaherty put up with my foibles in the most amazing way. Once he asked me if I wouldn't include some folk music. I refused. He said, "It was good enough for Dvorak, so it should be good enough for you." Out of the arrogance of youth, I answered, "I think we can do better than that!"

136. See William T. Murphy, *Robert Flaherty: A Guide to References and Resources*, 35–36, for an account of the conflict surrounding the film's release.

137. For an account of his few activities, see Rotha, ed. Ruby, 230–33; for a brief account of an unrealized film project in 1941, see James M. Linton, "Robert Flaherty's Unrealized Film on Jack Miner," in *Robert Flaherty: Photographer/Filmmaker, the Inuit, 1910–1922*, ed. Jo-Anne Birnie Danzker, 81–82.

138. Rotha, ed. Ruby, 237, wrote: "It was without question the most generous and favorable assignment any producer of documentary films has ever had. But who shall say that Flaherty did not deserve it? He had waited long enough for such confidence in his artistry."

139. In Rotha, ed. Ruby, 236, Frances Flaherty is quoted: "Bob was insistent that no one should show any affection for the boy except himself. He wanted sole control over him, as he had done with Sabu and Mikeleen."

140. Portions of her diary are printed in Rotha, ed. Ruby, 238–51; the manuscript is in the Film Study Center of the Museum of Modern Art, New York City. Of particular interest to this issue of collaboration is *A Film Study of Robert Flaherty's "Louisiana Story."* A compilation film, assembled under the direction of George Amberg and narrated by Frances Flaherty and Richard Leacock, this is a misguided effort to preserve a small part of the outtake footage and to discredit the contributions made to the film by Helen Van Dongen, whose name is not mentioned. It achieves precisely the opposite effect, revealing both Flaherty's casual shooting methods and Van Dongen's precise sense of cinematic form and rhythm. It is significant that there is no printed record of Robert Flaherty ever having disparaged her work and that the film was made after his death. For other accounts of the film's production, see Robert Flaherty, "Making a Film in the Louisiana Bayous," *Travel*, 92, No. 5 (May 1949), 13–15; Arnold Eagle, "Looking Back at *The Pirogue Maker, Louisiana Story*, and the Flaherty Way," *Film Library Quarterly*, 9, No. 1 (1976), 28–37; John Malcolm Brinnin, "The Flahertys: Pioneer Documentary Filmmakers,"

Harper's Bazaar, 81, No. 12 (December 1947), 146–47ff; and Ralph Rosenblum, *When the Shooting Stops . . . The Cutting Begins: A Film Editor's Story* (New York: Penguin, 1979), 112–21.

141. Flaherty introduces a potent mythic factor here. A superstition holds that a werewolf is a person who undergoes a change into a wolf, eats human flesh or drinks human blood, and then returns to his natural form. Alexander fears the invasion of "his" bayou (his personal territory; in that sense, his body). Like a man being transformed into a werewolf, the men on the oil rig undergo a change: they are calm at first, frenetic when drilling the oil, and calm again when they leave the bayou. Alexander uses his talisman against this invasion, and is happy again only when the men leave.

142. This image foreshadows a similar one in Michelangelo Antonioni's *The Red Desert* (1964) where a ship's prow invades the desolate industrial landscape.

143. In *The Techniques of Film Editing,* 155, Van Dongen writes: "The composition of the drilling sequence as a whole was conceived from the very beginning *with* the sound as an element of equal significance." The development of this sequence is explained and illustrated with sequential still photographs, 144–55.

144. Murphy, 41, says, Flaherty remained "at heart a silent filmmaker."

145. The clear logic of the editing of this industrial maneuver reflects Van Dongen's application of the aesthetics of Soviet silent film montage to several of the films that she edited for Joris Ivens, notably *Zuider Zee* (1933) and *New Earth* (1934).

146. See Rotha, ed. Ruby, 240, for Van Dongen's account of the problems encountered in shooting the scenes with alligators.

147. Apparently, the editing of this sequence created for Flaherty and his crew more problems than any other sequence in the film, exacerbated by a growing conflict between Frances Flaherty and Helen Van Dongen (this resulted in Van Dongen's departure from Louisiana for three weeks), and finally convinced Flaherty that he could not complete the picture without his editor. See Calder-Marshall, Chap. 17; Rotha, ed. Ruby, 246; Van Dongen's complete unpublished diary, Film Study Center, Museum of Modern Art.

148. In Rotha, ed. Ruby, 244–45, Van Dongen writes: "*Believe-it-or-not department:* it takes trappers years to learn how to hook alligators and it's a pretty dangerous job. When we planned this sequence, we decided to have Lionel LeBlanc [the father] come in very early. However, on the day of the shooting, Lionel was not available and, credible or not, J.L. [the boy] *did* pull in that alligator alone, though in an unorthodox way. We did *not* stage the scene."

149. Incidentally, Mrs. Latour, who has little significance, like the other women in Flaherty's films, seems much younger than her husband who, in any case, greatly resembles Flaherty himself. Flaherty wrote specific dialogue for this scene (as well as for earlier ones in the film in which there is dialogue), which was shot with a synchronous picture-sound camera. But the "actors" were "real" people, both camera-shy and unfamiliar with speaking words not their own; in addition, the dialogue is not particularly realistic, and they were unable, through successive takes, using different camera angles and lenses, to repeat themselves exactly. This creates problems both for the editor and the viewer. Faced with the difficulty of producing a lively scene from footage in which the picture-sound relationship was different in each take, Van Dongen experimented with a variety of techniques; see "Three Hundred and Fifty Cans of Film," 64–67. The problem is of course inherent in any film using real people instead of actors who are trained to remember their lines and who, in any event, are reminded by a script supervisor about such matters as physical placement and gesture in re-takes. Flaherty was successful in coaching these people in facial expressions and physical movement, but he was far less successful in

writing and in coaching the dialogue. The result is an artificial and stilted scene, all the more out of place in a film of such lyrical fluidity and natural beauty. See Rotha, ed. Ruby, 259–60.

150. Van Dongen disliked the awkward device of this letter; see Rotha, ed. Ruby, 247.

151. Calder-Marshall, 228, and Rotha, ed. Ruby, 236, reveal that Joseph Boudreaux, the boy who played Alexander, eventually became an oil driller.

152. For John Cage's excellent analysis of Thomson's score, see Kathleen Hoover and John Cage, *Virgil Thomson: His Life and Music* (New York: Yoseloff, 1959), 207–12; see also Roger Manvell and John Huntley, *The Technique of Film Music* (London: Focal, 1957), 99–109.

153. For the film, the score was played by the Philadelphia Orchestra under the direction of Eugene Ormandy. Thomson was further pleased that the two suites that he extracted from the film score have been played more than any other of his orchestral works.

154. For Van Dongen's comments on the challenge involved, see "Robert J. Flaherty: 1884–1951," 225.

155. The first is quoted in Van Dongen's diary (12 Sept. 1946), Film Study Center, Museum of Modern Art; the second in Rotha, ed. Ruby, 5.

156. Since editing is, in part, also the art of exclusion, this remark may also be an appreciative reference to what he had learned from his collaborators, particularly his editor.

157. The film, originally directed by Ernest Marischka, was presented in this country in prestige art houses with this credit: "Robert Flaherty Presents." The contract requires only the use of Flaherty's name, and he seems to have had nothing else to do with preparing this film for American release. The film includes about one-fourth of Bach's oratorio, performed by Herbert van Karajan conducting the Vienna Philharmonic, and featuring various soloists, including Elisabeth Schwarzkopf; this footage is intercut with shots of fifteenth-, sixteenth-, and seventeenth-century masterpieces of religious painting from various European museums. The film was released close to the time of Flaherty's death, and was used in at least two memorial services, both of which also included musical performances by the Trapp Family Singers.

158. Grierson observes that there were both positive and negative attributes to this neo-Rousseauism *(Grierson on Documentary* 148).

159. See Richard Barsam, *Filmguide to "Triumph of the Will"* (Bloomington: Indiana University Press, 1975).

160. André Bazin, *"Los Olvidados," The World of Luis Buñuel: Essays in Criticism,* ed. Joan Mellen (New York: Oxford University Press, 1978), 199; see also E. Rubinstein, "Visit to a Familiar Planet: Buñuel among the Hurdanos," *Cinema Journal* 22, No. 4 (Summer 1983), 3–17.

161. Stephen Mamber suggests that Flaherty influenced the development of direct cinema; see his *Cinema Verite in America: Studies in Uncontrolled Documentary* (Cambridge: The MIT Press, 1974), 9–14.

162. See Richard Barsam, "American Direct Cinema: The *Re*-Presentation of Reality." *Persistence of Vision,* Nos. 3–4 (Summer 1986), 131–56.

163. Custen writes:

His was a highly selected narrative universe in which mythic-like struggles of individuals took the place of a broader social criticism. Thus, Flaherty's self-acknowledged role of "explorer first, filmmaker second" obviates the larger social conscience Grierson and his followers felt was so critical to documentary film. As Claude Lévi-Strauss has noted, anthropologists and explorers, whatever their "private" motives, are treating members of their race as objects of domination and scrutiny. Despite Flaherty's genuine concern for the dignity of the people he filmed, his cinematic political conscience never extended beyond a class of one character in one film. (90)

164. Karl G. Heider, *Ethnographic Film* (Austin: University of Texas Press, 1976), 20–26; see also Ruby, "The Aggie Will Come First," 71, for a definition of Flaherty as ethnographer as well as for Margaret Mead's remarks on Flaherty's films.

165. Claude Lévi-Strauss suggests that audiences want to satisfy the "cannibal instincts of the historical process" to which, in this case, the Inuit had already surrendered; see *Tristes Tropiques,* trans. John Russell (New York: Criterion, 1961), 43.

166. Kracauer's and Bazin's theories about cinematic realism (written *a posteriori* and published after Flaherty's death) and their critical application of them to Flaherty's work provide a framework for understanding the films.

WORKS CITED

Achtenberg, Ben. "Helen Van Dongen: An Interview." *Film Quarterly,* 30.2 (Winter 1976): 46–57.

Alexander, William. *Film on the Left: American Documentary Film from 1931 to 1942.* Princeton: Princeton University Press, 1981.

Andrew, Dudley. *André Bazin.* New York: Oxford University Press, 1978.

Anstey, Edgar. "Development of Film Technique in Britain." *Experiment in the Film.* Ed. Roger Manvell. New York: Arno, 1970. 234–65.

Arnell, Richard. "Composing Music for *The Land.*" In Mike Weaver, *Robert Flaherty's "The Land."* Exeter, England: American Arts Documentation Centre, 1979. 11–14.

Balcon, Michael, et al. *Twenty Years of British Film: 1925–1947.* London: Falcon, 1947.

Barnouw, Erik. *Documentary: A History of the Non-Fiction Film.* New York: Oxford University Press, 1974.

———. "Robert Flaherty (Barnouw's File)." *Film Culture* 53–55 (Spring 1972): 161–85.

Barr, Alfred. *Picasso: Fifty Years of His Art.* New York: Museum of Modern Art, 1974.

Barry, Iris. *Let's Go to the Pictures.* London: Chatto, 1926.

Barsam, Richard. "American Direct Cinema: The *Re*-Presentation of Reality." *Persistence of Vision* 3–4 (Summer 1986): 131–56.

———. *Filmguide to "Triumph of the Will."* Bloomington: Indiana University Press, 1975.

———. *Nonfiction Film: A Critical History.* New York: Dutton, 1973.

———. "Nonfiction Film: The Realist Impulse." *Film Theory and Criticism.* Ed. Gerald Mast and Marshall Cohen. 2nd ed. New York: Oxford University Press, 1979. 580–93.

———, ed. *Nonfiction Film Theory and Criticism.* New York: Dutton, 1976.

Bazin, André. "*Los Olvidados.*" *The World of Luis Buñuel: Essays in Criticism.* Ed. Joan Mellen. New York: Oxford University Press, 1978. 194–200.

———. *What Is Cinema?* 2 vols. Berkeley: University of California Press, 1967.

Brinnin, John Malcolm. "The Flahertys: Pioneer Documentary Filmmakers." *Harper's Bazaar* Dec. 1947: 146–47.

Brownlow, Kevin. *The War, the West, and the Wilderness.* New York: Knopf, 1979.

Calder-Marshall, Arthur. *The Innocent Eye: The Life of Robert J. Flaherty.* New York: Harcourt, 1963.

Callenbach, Ernest. "The Understood Antagonist and Other Observations." *Film Quarterly* 12.4 (Summer 1959): 16–23.

"Campaign Book for Exhibitors." *Studies in Visual Communication* 6.2 (Summer 1980): 61–76.

Canby, Vincent. "Film: Olmi's *The Tree of Wooden Clogs* Opens." *New York Times* 1 June 1979, sec. c: 8.

Carpenter, Edmund, ed. *Anerca: Drawings by Enooesweetok.* Toronto: Dent, 1959.

———. *Eskimo.* Toronto: University of Toronto Press, 1959.

Clarke, Donald H. "Producer of *Nanook* Joins Metro-Goldwyn." *New York Times* 26 June 1927, sec. 8: 2.

Clurman, Harold. "Flaherty's *Louisiana Story*." *The Documentary Tradition*. Ed. Lewis Jacobs. New York: Hopkinson, 1971. 230–32.

Connolly, Cyril. *The Unquiet Grave*. New York: Harper, 1973.

Corliss, Richard. "Robert Flaherty: The Man in the Iron Myth." *Nonfiction Film Theory and Criticism*. Ed. Richard Meran Barsam. New York: Dutton, 1976. 230–38.

Custen, George F. "The (Re)framing of Robert Flaherty." *Quarterly Review of Film Studies* 7.1 (Winter 1982): 87–94.

Danzker, Jo-Anne Birnie. "Robert Flaherty/Photographer." *Studies in Visual Communication* 6.2 (Summer 1980): 5–32.

———, ed. *Robert Flaherty: Photographer/Filmmaker, the Inuit, 1910–1922*. Vancouver: Vancouver Art Gallery, 1980.

Dobi, Steve. "Restoring Robert Flaherty's *Nanook of the North*." *Film Library Quarterly* 10.1–2 (1977): 6–18.

Dratfield, Leo. "Robert Flaherty's Daughter Remembers: An Interview with Frances Flaherty Rohr." *Sightlines* (Fall/Winter 1984/85): 11–14.

Eagle, Arnold. "Looking Back . . . at *The Pirogue Maker, Louisiana Story,* and the Flaherty Way." *Film Library Quarterly* 9.1 (1976): 28–37.

Eisner, Lotte H. *Murnau*. Berkeley: University of California Press, 1973.

Fieschi, Jean-André. "F. W. Murnau." *Cinema: A Critical Dictionary*. Ed. Richard Roud. 2 vols. New York: Viking, 1980. 704–20.

Flaherty, David. "Serpents in Eden." *Asia* (Oct. 1925): 858–69.

Flaherty, Frances Hubbard. "A Search for Animal [sic] and Sea Sequence." *Asia* (Nov. 1925): 954–62.

———. "Behind the Scenes with Our Samoan Stars." *Asia* (Sept. 1925): 747–53.

———. *Elephant Dance*. New York: Scribner's, 1937.

———. "Explorations." *Film Book I: The Audience and the Filmmaker*. Ed. Robert Hughes. New York: Grove, 1959.

———. "Fa'A-Samoa." *Asia* (Dec. 1925): 1085–90.

———. "How *Man of Aran* Came into Being." *Film News* 13.3 (1953): 4–6.

———. *Sabu: The Elephant Boy*. New York: Oxford University Press, 1937.

———. *Samoa*. Berlin: Hobbing, 1932.

———. "Setting up House and Shop in Samoa." *Asia* (Aug. 1925): 639–51.

———. "The Camera's Eye." In George C. Pratt, *Spellbound in Darkness: A History of the Silent Film*. New York: New York Graphic, 1973. 344–47.

———. *The Odyssey of a Film-Maker: Robert Flaherty's Story*. New York: Arno, 1972.

Flaherty, Robert. "Account of Making the Film—*Man of Aran*." Box 31. Flaherty Papers. Columbia University, New York.

———. "Acoma." Box 28. Flaherty Papers. Columbia University, New York.

———. "Craftesmanship [sic]." Box 28. Flaherty Papers. Columbia University, New York.

———. "Filming Real People." *The Documentary Tradition: From Nanook to Woodstock*. Ed. Lewis Jacobs. New York: Hopkinson, 1971. 97–99.

———. "How I Filmed *Nanook of the North*." *Film Makers on Film Making*. Ed. Harry M. Geduld. Bloomington: Indiana University Press, 1971. 56–64.

———. "Life among the Eskimos." *The World's Work* Oct. 1922: 632–40.

———. "Making a Film in the Louisiana Bayous." *Travel* May 1949: 13–15.

———. "*Man of Aran* Programs." Box 31. Flaherty Papers. Columbia University, New York.

——. *My Eskimo Friends*. Garden City: Doubleday, 1924.

——. "Nanook." *The Emergence of Film Art*. Ed. Lewis Jacobs. New York: Hopkinson, 1969.

——. "Picture Making in the South Seas." *Film Daily Yearbook—1924*: 9–13.

——. "Robert Flaherty Talking." *The Cinema 1950*. Ed. Roger Manvell. London: Penguin, 1950. 11–29.

——. "Robert Flaherty Tells How He Made *Man of Aran*." *National Board of Review Magazine* Jan. 1935: 5–7.

——. "Tabu, A Story of the South Seas." *Film Culture* 20 (1959): 27–38.

——. "The Belcher Islands of Hudson Bay: Their Discovery and Exploration." *Geographical Review* 5.6 (1918): 433–58.

——. *The Captain's Chair: A Story of the North*. New York: Scribner's, 1938.

——. "The Most Unforgettable Character I've Met." *Reader's Digest* Mar. 1942: 41–44.

——. "Turia, An Original Story." *Film Culture* 20 (1959): 17–26.

——. "Two Traverses across Ungava Peninsula, Labrador." *Geographical Review* 6.2 (1918): 116–32.

——. "Wetalltook's Islands." *The World's Work* Feb. 1923: 422–33.

——. *White Master*. London: Routledge, 1939.

——. "Winter on Wetalltook's Islands." *The World's Work* Mar. 1923: 538–53.

Freud, Sigmund. *Civilization and Its Discontents*. Trans. and Ed. James Strachey. New York: Norton, 1962.

Goldstein, Laurence, and Jay Kaufman. *Into Film*. New York: Dutton, 1976.

Goodman, Ezra. "Pioneer's Return: Robert Flaherty Discusses His Latest Documentary, *The Louisiana Story* [sic]." *New York Times* 31 Aug. 1947, sec. 2: 3.

Gray, Hugh. "Father of the American Documentary." *The American Cinema*. Ed. Donald E. Staples. Washington: U.S. Information Agency, 1973. 191–212.

——. "Robert Flaherty and the Naturalistic Documentary." *Hollywood Quarterly* 5.1 (Fall 1950): 41–48.

Grierson, John. "Elephant Boy." *World Film News* 1.12 (Mar. 1937): 5.

——. "Flaherty as Innovator." *Sight and Sound* 21.2 (Oct.-Dec. 1951): 64–68.

——. "Flaherty's Poetic *Moana*." *The Documentary Tradition: From Nanook to Woodstock*. Ed. Lewis Jacobs. New York: Hopkinson, 1971. 27–28.

——. *Grierson on Documentary*. Ed. Forsyth Hardy. London: Faber, 1966.

——. "Robert Flaherty." n.d., n.p. Flaherty File, Film Study Center, Museum of Modern Art, New York.

Griffith, Richard. "Flaherty and *Tabu*." *Film Culture* 20 (1959): 12–13.

——. *The World of Robert Flaherty*. New York: Duell, 1953.

Hardy, Forsyth. *John Grierson: A Documentary Biography*. London: Faber, 1979.

Heider, Karl G. *Ethnographic Film*. Austin: University of Texas Press, 1976.

Hoover, Kathleen and John Cage. *Virgil Thomson: His Life and Music*. New York: Yoseloff, 1959.

Houston, Penelope. "Interview with Flaherty." *Sight and Sound* Jan. 1950: 16.

Jacobs, Lewis. *The Rise of the American Film*. New York: Columbia University Teachers College Press, 1968.

Kipling, Rudyard. "Toomai of the Elephants." *The Jungle Books*. Garden City: Doubleday, 1948. Vol. 2: 145–72.

Korda, Michael. *Charmed Lives: A Family Romance*. New York: Random, 1979.

Kracauer, Siegfried. *Theory of Film: The Redemption of Physical Reality*. New York: Oxford University Press, 1960.

Kraus, Robert, ed. *Nanook of the North*. New York: Windmill, 1971.

Kulik, Karol. *Alexander Korda: The Man Who Could Work Miracles*. New Rochelle: Arlington, 1975.

Langer, Mark J. "*Tabu*: The Making of a Film." *Cinema Journal* 24.3 (Spring 1985): 43–64.

Leacock, Richard. "*Moana* with Music." *Sight and Sound* 54.1 (Winter 1984–85): 4–5.

Leaming, Barbara. *Orson Welles: A Biography*. New York: Penguin, 1986.

Levin, G. Roy. *Documentary Explorations: Fifteen Interviews with Film-makers*. Garden City: Doubleday, 1971.

Lévi-Strauss, Claude. *Tristes Tropiques*. Trans. John Russell. New York: Criterion, 1961.

Linton, James M. "Robert Flaherty's Unrealized Film on Jack Miner." *Robert Flaherty: Photographer/Filmmaker, the Inuit, 1910–1922*. Ed. Jo-Anne Birnie Danzker. Vancouver: Vancouver Art Gallery, 1980. 81–82.

Lord, Russell. *Behold Our Land*. Boston: Houghton, 1938.

———. "Robert Flaherty Rediscovers America: Editorial Notes and Forthcoming Motion Picture." *The Land* 1.1 (Winter 1941): 67–75.

Lord, Russell, and Kate [Lord]. *Forever the Land*. New York: Harper, 1950.

Lorentz, Pare. *Lorentz on Film: Movies 1927 to 1941*. New York: Hopkinson, 1975.

MacCann, Richard Dyer. *The People's Films: A Political History of U.S. Government Motion Pictures*. New York: Hastings, 1973.

Mainwaring, Mary Louise. "Robert Flaherty's Films and Their Critics." Diss. Indiana University, 1954.

Malinowski, Bronislaw. *Argonauts of the Western Pacific*. New York: Dutton, 1922.

Mamber, Stephen. *Cinema Verite in America: Studies in Uncontrolled Documentary*. Cambridge: The MIT Press, 1974.

Manvell, Roger, and John Huntley. *The Technique of Film Music*. London: Focal, 1957.

Mast, Gerald. *A Short History of the Movies*. 3rd ed. Indianapolis: Bobbs-Merrill, 1981.

Mead, Margaret, and Gregory Bateson. "Margaret Mead and Gregory Bateson on the Use of the Camera in Anthropology." *Studies in Visual Communication* 4.2 (Winter 1977): 78–80.

Mullen, Pat. *Man of Aran*. Cambridge: The MIT Press, 1970.

Munden, Kenneth, ed. *The American Film Institute Catalog of Motion Pictures Produced in the United States: Feature Films 1921–1930*. 2 vols. New York: Bowker, 1971.

Murphy, William T. *Robert Flaherty: A Guide to References and Resources*. Boston: Hall, 1978.

O'Brien, Frederick. *White Shadows in the South Seas*. New York: Century, 1919.

Pratt, George C. *Spellbound in Darkness: A History of the Silent Film*. New York: New York Graphic Society, 1973.

Ramsaye, Terry. "Flaherty, Great Adventurer." In George C. Pratt, *Spellbound in Darkness: A History of the Silent Film*. New York: New York Graphic Society, 1973. 342–54.

Reisz, Karel, and Gavin Miller. *The Technique of Film Editing*. New York: Farrar, 1953.

Renoir, Jean. *My Life and My Films*. New York: Atheneum, 1974.

Richards, Jeffrey. *Visions of Yesterday*. London: Routledge, 1973.

Rosenblum, Ralph, with Robert Karen. *When the Shooting Stops . . .the Cutting Begins: A Film Editor's Story*. New York: Penguin, 1979.

Rosenheimer, Arthur [pseud. Arthur Knight]. "They Make Documentaries: Number One—Robert Flaherty." *Film News* 7.6 (Apr. 1946): 1–23.

Rotha, Paul. *Documentary Diary: An Informal History of the British Documentary Film, 1928–1939*. New York: Hill, 1973.

———. *Documentary Film*. New York: Hastings, 1952.

————. *Robert J. Flaherty: A Biography.* Ed. Jay Ruby. Philadelphia: University of Pennsylvania Press, 1983.

Rotha, Paul, and Basil Wright. "Flaherty Biography Mss." Library, Museum of Modern Art, New York. Also Box 69. Flaherty Papers. Columbia University, New York.

————. "Nanook of the North." *Studies in Visual Communication* 6.2 (Summer 1980): 33–60.

Rouse, John Thomas, Jr. "A Descriptive Analysis of the Major Films of Robert J. Flaherty." Diss. University of Michigan, 1968.

Rubinstein, E. "Visit to a Familiar Planet: Buñuel among the Hurdanos." *Cinema Journal* 22.4 (Summer 1983): 3–17.

Ruby, Jay. "The Aggie Will Come First: The Demystification of Robert Flaherty." *Robert Flaherty: Photographer/Filmmaker, the Inuit, 1910–1922.* Ed. Jo-Anne Birnie Danzker. Vancouver: Vancouver Art Gallery, 1980. 66–73.

Sarris, Andrew. *The American Cinema: Directors and Directions, 1929–1968.* New York: Dutton, 1963.

Shepard, David. "Authenticating Films." *The Quarterly Journal of the Library of Congress* 37.3–4 (Summer-Fall 1980): 342–54.

Snyder, Robert L. *Pare Lorentz and the Documentary Film.* Norman: University of Oklahoma Press, 1968.

Stefansson, Vilhjalmur. *The Standardization of Error.* London: Kegan, 1929.

Strauss, Theodore. "The Giant Shinnies down the Beanstalk: Flaherty's *The Land.*" *The Documentary Tradition: From Nanook to Woodstock.* Ed. Lewis Jacobs. New York: Hopkinson, 1971. 197–99.

Sussex, Elizabeth. *The Rise and Fall of British Documentary: The Story of the Film Movement Founded by John Grierson.* Berkeley: University of California Press, 1975.

Synge, J. M. *Riders to the Sea. A Treasury of the Theatre.* Ed. John Gassner. New York: Simon, 1960. 628–732.

————. *The Aran Islands.* Boston: Luce, 1911.

Szarkowski, John. *Looking at Photographs.* New York: Museum of Modern Art, 1973.

Thomson, Virgil. *Virgil Thomson.* New York: Knopf, 1966.

Troy, William. "Films: Behind the Scenes." *The Nation* 10 July 1935: 56.

————. "Film: Pure Cinema." *The Nation* 31 Oct. 1934: 518.

Van Dongen, Helen. "Notebooks of Helen Van Dongen." Mss. Film Study Center, Museum of Modern Art, New York.

————. "Robert J. Flaherty: 1884–1951." *Nonfiction Film Theory and Criticism.* Ed. Richard M. Barsam. New York: Dutton, 1976. 212–29.

————. "Three Hundred and Fifty Cans of Film." *Cinema 1951.* London: Penguin, 1951. 57–78.

Vidal, Gore. "Rich Kids." Rev. of *Privileged Ones* by Robert Coles. *New York Review of Books* 9 Feb. 1978: 9–14.

Weaver, Mike. *Robert Flaherty's "The Land."* Exeter, England: American Arts Documentation Centre, University of Exeter, 1979.

Werner, P. "Frances Flaherty: Hidden and Seeking." *Film Makers' Newsletter* July-Aug. 1972: 28–30.

White, William L. "Pare Lorentz." *Scribner's* Jan. 1939: 7–11.

Williams, Christopher, ed. *Realism and the Cinema.* London: Routledge, 1980.

Winston, Brian. "The White Man's Burden: The Example of Robert Flaherty." *Sight and Sound* 54.1 (Winter 1984–85): 58–60.

INDEX